THE
Comet
& THE
Tornado

Reflections on the Legacy of
RANDY PAUSCH, *The Last Lecture*
& the Creation of Our Carnegie Mellon
Dream Fulfillment Factory

DON MARINELLI

STERLING

New York / London
www.sterlingpublishing.com

STERLING and the distinctive Sterling logo are registered trademarks of Sterling Publishing Co., Inc.

Library of Congress Cataloging-in-Publication Data

Marinelli, Don.
   The comet & the tornado: reflections on the legacy of Randy Pausch, the last lecture, and the creation of our Carnegie Mellon dream fulfillment factory / Don Marinelli.
           p. cm.
   The comet and the tornado
   ISBN 978-1-4027-7088-3
   1. Entertainment computing—United States. 2. Entertainment technology—United States. 3. Pausch, Randy. 4. Computer scientists—United States—Biography. I. Title. II. Title: The Comet and the Tornado.
   QA76.9.E57M37 2010
   790.20285—dc22

                          2009036509

10 9 8 7 6 5 4 3 2 1

Published by Sterling Publishing Co., Inc.
387 Park Avenue South, New York, NY 10016
© 2010 by Don Marinelli
Distributed in Canada by Sterling Publishing
c/o Canadian Manda Group, 165 Dufferin Street
Toronto, Ontario, Canada M6K 3H6
Distributed in the United Kingdom by GMC Distribution Services
Castle Place, 166 High Street, Lewes, East Sussex, England BN7 1XU
Distributed in Australia by Capricorn Link (Australia) Pty. Ltd.
P.O. Box 704, Windsor, NSW 2756, Australia

This book is a memoir. It reflects the author's present recollection of his experiences that occurred over a period of years, and dialogue has been recreated from memory. All emails are printed with permission of the sender.

Design by Anderson Design Group, AndersonDesignGroup.com

Sterling ISBN 978-1-4027-7088-3

For information about custom editions, special sales, premium and corporate purchases, please contact Sterling Special Sales Department at 800.805.5489 or specialsales@sterlingpublishing.com.

This book is dedicated to the memory of
Paul Christiano, Anne Humphreys,
Akram Midani & Randy Pausch

Contents

Introduction

First came the Tornado.

Randy Pausch, my cofounder and partner in crime at the Carnegie Mellon Entertainment Technology Center (the ETC in short), gave me that name during his famous Last Lecture of September 2007. I recall hearing him use the term while I was sitting in a hotel room in Taipei, Taiwan, watching the lecture on my laptop in the middle of a typhoon (more on that later), and smiling instantly. The description fit my personality perfectly, though I'd never thought about myself in quite that meteorological term.

In sitting down to write this book, I began thinking, trying to come up with a one-word description of Randy. I reflected on the amazing journey he had taken as his Last Lecture grew into a veritable phenomenon. This talk, given at Carnegie Mellon before a crowd of friends, colleagues, former and current students, well-wishers, and others, quickly reached people worldwide, thanks to the power of the Internet and the *Wall Street Journal*, in which Carnegie Mellon alumnus and reporter Jeff Zaslow dedicated an article to the amazing happening at his alma mater.

At first I likened Randy to a *rocket ship* because of the ascendancy he experienced once millions of perfect strangers were able to watch his Last Lecture on YouTube. The name seemed to make perfect sense, and was in keeping with his childhood interests. (He'd painted a rocket on his bedroom wall as a child—and the book version of his lecture features a rocket on its cover.)

Then as I reflected on how Randy's words of wisdom illuminated life for so many people around the world, the word *meteoric* came to mind. Yet while a meteor seemed more apropos than a rocket ship, it still fell short of capturing the Randy phenomenon. Think like a scientist for a moment. A meteor either burns up upon entering the earth's atmosphere or falls to earth as a meteorite; meteorites can be found, retrieved, and examined. Meteorites are, by definition, finite. No, Randy far transcended that description.

So, if I wanted to stick with some kind of astral nickname for Randy, the best fit was *comet*. And that word has additional resonance, too, given that Randy tells a story in the Last Lecture about his great childhood dream of experiencing zero gravity—a dream realized years later, when he flew in what NASA lovingly refers to as the "Vomit Comet."

Comet Pausch burst upon the scene like an astral body illuminating the sky; he created an amazing glow and presence in the heavens, sharing his secrets for living life to the fullest with millions of folks who needed such guidance. Then, this amazingly beautiful comet hurtled off into the universe.

Like his astronomical namesake, Comet Pausch left millions of people stunned, amazed, happy, giddy, and seeing light where there had been only darkness. He inspired great hope and genuine resolve in a way seldom equaled by politicians, movie stars, writers, television personalities, motivators, and teachers.

There is another reason, though, why I find this term for Randy so appropriate. One of my favorite novels is *In the Days of the Comet*, by the famous English social commentator, historian, and science fiction genius H. G. Wells. In this fantasy, the earth passes through the tail of a passing comet. The result is nothing less than a catalytic change. The world is transformed from the bickering, dysfunctional, self-centered place we know all too well to a place more closely resembling Utopia, where all of humankind works together to improve the quality of life for everyone on the planet.

In the Days of the Comet concludes with an epilogue in which Wells's protagonist realizes the profundity of the change:

> It was more and more evident to me that this was a different
> humanity from any I had known, unreal, having different customs,

different beliefs, different interpretations, different emotions. It was no mere change in conditions and institutions the comet had wrought. It had made a change of heart and mind.

That seems like the most apt description of the impact that my friend and colleague had on our world during his year and a half of international prominence.

I like to think Comet Pausch remains aglow in the heavens. He most definitely remains alive on YouTube, in the best-selling book version of the lecture, in the memories of his students, friends, and colleagues.

The ETC has memorialized Randy in the renaming of its primary classroom, in the creation of an award for a deserving ETC student, and in the establishment of the Pausch Prize for entertainment technology industry professionals who have successfully bridged the false divide between science and art. Carnegie Mellon has named the footbridge connecting the Gates Center for Computer Science and the Purnell Center for the Arts in honor of Randy; and the Human-Computer Interaction Institute renamed its laboratory complex in his honor as well.

But the true homage to Randy, in my opinion, lies within the Carnegie Mellon Entertainment Technology Center. In his Last Lecture, Randy refers to the ETC as the Carnegie Mellon "Dream Fulfillment Factory." I like this moniker. You see, I'm a man of the theater, and hardly anyone enters theater because his parents made him do so. As a theater person, I am quite used to dreamers—but the ETC certainly introduced me to a wider variety of them. Randy helped me understand those dreams that originate on the other side of the brain—the left side. In my work there, I met people who were different from me in many ways, yet similar. I encountered the *yin* and the *yang* of youth. I landed in a strange land only to discover I was right at home.

It is essential that Randy's message continue to resonate and exert impact on the world. His intention was to impart lessons learned in a life lived to the fullest, a life lived even more intentionally and feverishly after he received his fatal diagnosis of pancreatic cancer.

This book is my attempt to recall, remember, reflect upon, and at times reconcile the years I spent working side by side with Randy Pausch, and with the Comet Randy phenomenon following the Last Lecture. It isn't that the two are different and distinct, but I have come to realize that the Comet was a transformation of the Randy I worked alongside of for six years.

The Comet's journey—as observed by the Tornado—and the educational legacy we created together are what this reflection is all about.

Don Marinelli
Pittsburgh, Fall 2009

Chapter One

What's a Drama Guy Like Me Doing in a Place Like This?

For fifteen years I worked in Carnegie Mellon's prestigious Department of Drama, first as its Assistant Head and then its Associate Head. I felt I had it made—at least within the world of theater academia. Carnegie Mellon boasts the oldest degree-granting drama program in the nation, accepting only the cream of the crop of young actors; musical theater aspirants; directors; stage managers; set, costume, lighting, and sound designers; and playwrights.

The department is ensconced in a magnificent classical structure bearing the hallowed name of The College of Fine Arts, and is believed to be the first college building in the country designed to house all of the arts programs under one roof. And what a roof it is. The foyer entrance branches off to the Department of Music's Alumni Concert Hall on one side and Drama's Kresge Theater on the other. Above milling patrons and students is a Sistine Chapel–like fresco depicting a gathering of giants from all the fine arts—Bach, Mozart, Da Vinci, Beethoven, Schilling, Goethe, and other historical luminaries—all placed amidst the landmarks of old Pittsburgh: steel mills, smokestacks, blast furnaces, bridges, and other technological marvels of the nineteenth and twentieth centuries. Surreal, yes, but it remains awe-inspiring.

The building is never without commotion: music students rehearsing, actors running lines, dancers timing steps, art students lost in their sketch pads, architecture students setting up exhibitions of their models . . . and

I was immersed in all of it for fifteen years, gleeful that my office opened onto a whirlwind of artistic enterprise.

But all was not right in my little paradise as we entered the final decade of the twentieth century. For some years, I had been feeling a growing sense of disconnection between the students we had been auditioning around the country and the art form we call theater. They seemed less and less motivated by the pure vocation of acting and more attracted to Hollywood glamour and show-business superficiality. When I asked applicants what they preferred to do on a Friday evening, fewer and fewer responded, "attend a play." More hands went up when I offered the suggestion, "play a video game."

Technology was making tremendous inroads at every level of society. Yet, I still had colleagues who were averse to using email because they perceived it as a fad, too complicated, or a "dehumanizing force." Sadly, there was nothing new about this antithetical stance toward popular culture.

I recall my first week at Carnegie Mellon in May 1981. I was getting to know the faculty and staff, introducing myself, conveying how excited I was to be part of this enterprise and my desire to be a positive addition to the department. One of the first faculty members I met, and someone who extended a genuine welcome, was the department's technical director, Fred Youens.

Fred was a no-nonsense TD. He smoked like a chimney, was always dressed in work clothes, and had been at Carnegie Mellon for decades. He was kind enough to give me the lay of the land as he saw it, and I listened intently. What really stood out for me in that first encounter with Fred was the bumper sticker he placed in my hands as a welcome gift of sorts:

Theater Is Life
Television Is Furniture

I quickly learned that this sentiment was widespread amongst my drama colleagues.

While I have never been a major television aficionado, I am absolutely aware and respectful of the cultural impact it has had on global society—to say nothing of its astounding financial impact as an industry. Neglecting that reality or, worse yet, underestimating television's relevance and importance, struck me as nothing short of insane. It was also astoundingly hypocritical because the Department of Drama, as well as Carnegie Mellon University itself, had taken to boasting of the accomplishments of alumni who had achieved fame and fortune in the medium. The expression "Don't bite the hand that feeds you" came to mind as I pondered this irony.

If the theater faculty seemed dismissive of television, you can only imagine their opinion of a much newer form of entertainment: video games. Talk of the devil! Right-wing religious extremists had absolutely nothing on theater academicians when it came to public disdain for video games. They were dismissed by many of my peers as unworthy of discussion, reflection, or consideration. I found this attitude socially arrogant and professionally ignorant.

Video games were at that time a marginal entertainment medium, but in that respect they were no different from early cinema. Watching Mary Pickford escape from her evil landlord only to be caught on an ice floe in a rushing river isn't exactly high art, but you would have had to be brain-dead not to see the potential of the medium. So the Department of Drama's steadfast refusal even to consider video games, or any other form of interactive entertainment, as a potential artistic and/or employment opportunity always struck me as nearsighted and self-destructive.

By the mid-1990s, this issue was becoming more pressing for me, exacerbated by the continuing evolution of my students' entertainment interests, as well as entertainment-related developments within the rapidly developing field of computer science.

Carnegie Mellon's School of Computer Science was one of the first in the country and is as renowned and influential as the School of Drama. It boasts an amazing pedigree born of the efforts and genius of such luminaries as Allen Newell, Nobel laureate Herbert Simon, and Alan J. Perlis. The department was officially formed in July 1965 with the mission to explore this new technology in all its forms. Its founders aspired to nothing short of establishing a new discipline called "computer science." In 1988, the Department of Computer

Science was officially elevated to the status of a *School* of Computer Science.

Still, the School of Computer Science was as foreign to me as the Department of Sanskrit Studies. I had no idea what they did there, save for the fact that it probably required lots of math, and I wasn't very good at math.

Interestingly enough, my computer science "experience" had actually commenced way back in 1982. That year, IBM and Carnegie Mellon reached an agreement whereby new contraptions called Personal Computers would be distributed throughout campus to department heads and administrators. As Assistant Head of Drama, I was qualified to get one.

I remember distinctly the day there was a knock on my office door and I opened it to confront a deliveryman holding two beige containers about the size of a bread box.

"This is for you," he said.

Not quite knowing what to make of the thing, I smiled blankly at him and motioned to my desk. He placed the larger box containing the computer on it, capped off by a smaller box containing a monitor. He connected some cables, grunted, and then handed me an "owner's manual" about the size of the Manhattan telephone book.

"What am I supposed to do with this?" I asked.

"Read it," he said before exiting.

Since I am not fond of reading small-print volumes the size of the Gutenberg Bible, I placed the new toy and its accompanying opus on a spare desk in the corner. And there they sat.

Some time in the new year I was called into the office of Akram Midani, the Dean of the College of Fine Arts. Akram was a mentor to me, almost an idol. He was a veritable genius—erudite, cunning, multilingual, a college *pasha*. He beckoned me to sit down and said, "Don, we have a problem."

Those are not words any departmental administrator wants to hear from the dean.

"We have reports that you are not using your computer," he said. It took me a moment to figure out that he was referring to the beige box collection in the corner of my office. Being an actor, I feigned affront, outrage, and shock at this indignity, declaring vociferously, "That is an absolute lie. I do use it!"

"You do?" he replied genuinely surprised.

"Yes," I went on, pausing for effect, "As a shelf."

We both laughed; but the point was made.

I went back to my office and attempted to understand the basics of these early personal computers. I discovered cumbersome software programs, a rudimentary dot matrix printer, and a hypnotic monochromatic green screen monitor. Watching that thing was like being forced to watch a medical monitor all day—except you found you were praying for it to flatline. As a result, I used the thing as sparingly as possible.

One of the delicious ironies of Carnegie Mellon is that it is now known as a university that embraces multidisciplinary studies—but that was *not* the case when I first arrived there. It was all about concentrating on your one true calling. In drama we auditioned hundreds of seventeen-year-olds each year, looking for those talented few obsessive-compulsive individuals who knew that if they didn't act on stage they would spontaneously combust, those few for whom greasepaint was the artistic equivalent of crack cocaine, for whom wearing dance shoes was preferable to wearing glass or ruby slippers. They flocked to us with their hopes, dreams, aspirations, and delusions, and we either nurtured them via the medieval master/apprentice relationship or weeded them out like a farmer wielding a scythe. I have often compared enrolling in Carnegie Mellon Drama to enlisting in the Marine Corps. You work your butt off, often regretting your decision, wondering where it is all leading . . . but if you survive the grueling endurance contest, you will truly become one of the few and the proud.

My introduction to the possible intersection of computer science and the arts occurred one day in 1987, when I received a telephone call from Scott Stevens. Scott was a senior member of the technical staff at the Software Engineering Institute (SEI) and was involved in something called the Advanced Learning Technologies (ALT) Project. I knew none of this at the time. All I knew was that the SEI served as a clearinghouse for all non-weapon-related software used by the military. Getting a call from anyone associated with SEI had me fearing sudden military call-up, and images of being sent to some far-off battleground popped into my head. Thankfully, the reason for the call had nothing to do with military service and everything to do with my profession.

Scott was in need of actors for a film being shot at SEI. Acting jobs! The opportunity for a drama student to play a part in a movie was manna from heaven. Scott described the scene he was casting, some sort of team meeting, and we got down to work.

"What are you looking for?" I inquired like some hotshot Hollywood agent, "Blondes, brunettes, redheads? You want young, old, short, tall, you name it, we got it." I admit I have always loved finding opportunities for students; I remember how appreciative I was, as a young drama student, when alerted to employment possibilities. Plus, I think I was enjoying playing the role of agent.

"How much should these actors be paid?" Scott asked in blissful ignorance. Sensing a chance to snatch some low-hanging fruit, I blurted out, "Oh, $100 for a day's work is the going rate." In 1987, that represented good money—so good that I fully expected Scott to push back. When he readily answered, "Oh, that's fine," I was ecstatic for the students who would get the gig, but it also made me wonder just how much money they had in the Software Engineering Institute.

I helped Scott find the talent he was looking for, thanked him profusely, and thought nothing more about it. To my amazement (and delight), Scott called back again and again looking for more actors. Finally, I inquired, "What exactly are you shooting?" wondering what kind of film needed so many actors, and so haphazardly.

Scott replied that he was making an *interactive laser disc* for a major government agency. The goal was to create a game (or simulation, as they preferred to call it) that would teach something called "code inspection" in an engaging manner. I don't know how I responded, but I was thinking, *What on earth is an interactive laser disc? And what in heaven's name is code inspection?* My curiosity piqued, I asked him more questions about his new technology: How did it work, what could it do, why was it of interest, what were its capabilities, who was funding it? Finally, he extended an invitation to come by and witness the technology in action.

The first thing I noticed was that the Software Engineering Institute facility resembled the *Starship Enterprise* of *Star Trek* fame. Scott had every technological bell and whistle imaginable, and he was applying these toys (I mean tools) to the creation of a *dramatic* environment that could be inhabited by multiple players/actors. It struck me as a new kind of improvisation or role-playing game, the kind we used in acting class, except within SEI, a place filled with the best and brightest computer scientists, programmers, engineers, and other technical geniuses. They needed actors to realize their grand technological vision. An intersection!

A seed had been planted, but it would be awhile before it took root. Scott and I didn't hook up again until eight years later, in what would turn out to be a very fateful encounter.

By 1995, Scott had become a research scientist in the School of Computer Science, working on something called Informedia—a searchable digital video database system. It was designed to be something like having your very own Blockbuster store. Sensing my interest, he invited me to come over and see the system in action, believing it had potential for entertainment industry applications. That's where he hoped I could provide some ideas, input, and Hollywood networking.

I can now admit publicly that up to that time I had never crossed the Carnegie Mellon "cut"—the pastel swath of green grass separating the east and west sides of the campus. The beloved "cut" is the Maginot Line between the science departments and the arts, a physical and botanical bifurcation of right-brain/left-brain pursuits. Given the turns my life has taken since then, it seems ironic, but up to that time I'd had no more reason to wander over to Computer Science than a fish would have to wander onto dry land.

Computer Science was housed in arguably one of the ugliest buildings ever constructed: Wean Hall, which looks like something Albert Speer, Hitler's favorite architect, would have been proud of designing. It resembles a bunker/bomb shelter/fortress, and is as inviting as one. I swear that when I first entered the building in the mid-1990s, I encountered translucent-skinned students who resembled deep-sea creatures that had never seen light.

Wending my way through the beige concrete-block hallways of Wean Hall, I finally located the Informedia Project. And what I saw in that lab confirmed for me that you can judge neither a book by its cover nor a technology by the building it is in! Informedia surpassed Scott's glowing description, combining speech, images, and natural language understanding to transcribe, segment, and index linear video automatically. The material was organized so that you could initiate intelligent searches and retrieve images instantly. What had always been done by hand, tediously, was now automated. I began imagining myriad uses for the technology. What struck me the most, however, was how it could be used to create new ways of telling stories—essentially new forms of drama.

I returned to my office excited about what I had seen. In the midst of this exaltation, however, were distinct feelings of concern and anxiety. What I had just witnessed represented quite a departure from my familiar life and focus on drama. The seeds of restlessness had been sown; a new future of artistic and business possibilities was opening up.

I soon became the John the Baptist of the Drama Department, extolling the tremendous possibilities of the technology I'd experienced in the School of Computer Science. I evangelized at faculty meetings, in the classroom, the faculty lounge, the faculty dining room, indeed any place I encountered an audience. I implored my drama colleagues to embrace these rapidly evolving technologies and explore how they could and surely *would* impact art and entertainment.

I recall vividly the impact of the 1993 blockbuster movie *Jurassic Park*, a landmark in the use of computer-generated imagery. Here was a film that could not have been made without the use of computers. And even more impressive was the public's reaction to *Jurassic Park*, which broke several existing box office records.

Shortly after that movie came out, I happened upon a small article buried in the back pages of *Variety*. The headline was something like, "Sonic the Hedgehog Sets New Sales Records for Sega." Who? What? Soon I was on a very steep and swift learning curve; I immersed myself in the video game industry. What I learned astounded me. A whole new industry had blossomed right under my stuck-up nose. Furthermore, an entire generation of young people had spoken: They were embracing video games and causing a true sea change in entertainment attitudes and predilections.

This would prove to be the Rubicon moment for me, brought on by a dinosaur movie and my new best friend, Sonic the Hedgehog.

Every chance I had, I brought up this paradigm shift to my drama colleagues, but the reaction was always the same: a condescending version of "that's nice." I delved into the skills necessary to make video games and computer-enhanced movies, but found no traction when I suggested reviewing, revising, or re-orienting our existing curriculum. All my enthusiasm seemed for naught. Nothing appeared to have changed since Fred Youens had given me that bumper sticker bemoaning the primacy of television in American society.

Around that time, a committee had been assembled within the department to contribute design ideas for our long-awaited new building. We were to be rechristened the School of Drama. I felt forlorn as heated discussions revolved around whether or not to include a video studio in the overall design. Perhaps that space would be better suited for additional acting and/or rehearsal space, ran the counter-argument.

I thought to myself, *Here we are debating whether to include the revolutionary technology of the twentieth century in our new building, even as we stand on the precipice of the twenty-first century. What is wrong with this picture?* The simple reality was that the digital technology revolution had already begun picking up speed. If anything, we were playing catch-up!

All suggestions to include a green screen studio (a requisite for special-effects compositing in cinema and video games) or even a computer cluster were met with varied and heated dissension. Cost was presented as a factor, although I perceived this was an excuse to cover up serious ideological mistrust (i.e. fear) of computer-enhanced media and the digitization of our innate art forms.

While traditions die hard in theater, some part of me was dying quickly in the course of these discussions. I started to believe that if I truly wanted to grow as an artist, a teacher, a leader, dare I say a visionary, then I needed to make a change. As I wondered who within the School of Drama could lead us into the twenty-first century, a time when art and technology would work in unison toward a shared aesthetic, I suddenly found myself looking in the mirror.

I had found in Carnegie Mellon's School of Computer Science a personal version of Willy Wonka's chocolate factory. I began to think the formerly unthinkable: How could I become part of this wonderland? One day, as nervous as I would have been asking the homecoming queen for a date, I inquired of Scott, "Do you think there is any room on the Informedia team for someone like me?"

I fully expected him to say, "Gee, Don, that is an interesting question, but tell me, what was your math score on the GRE?" or "That's great Don, I've been looking for someone to help me with local search, tabu search, and simulated annealing algorithms." At which point I would walk away, embarrassed, directly into the path of an oncoming bus on Forbes Avenue.

What Scott actually said was, "I think it would be a great idea for you to join our team. Why don't I bring it up with Howard? If he is positive about it, then you and he can talk directly."

Howard Wactlar served as the principal investigator of the Informedia Project. I knew of him because he and his wife were loyal subscribers to the School of Drama mainstage season. Howard was a Renaissance man who loved theater and the arts, and he was a true gentleman. Scott got back to me quickly, with the go-ahead to call Howard.

I was terrified making that phone call. I really didn't know what I was asking of Howard other than a chance to play in his technology sandbox. When his kind and friendly voice came on the line I felt myself thrust suddenly into some kind of academic confessional. It was as though he had been transformed into Father Howard and I into a desperate penitent. I explained my situation to him, my desire to open myself to new things, to reinvent myself by expanding into other disciplines. His response changed my life. Instead of dismissing me, Howard was enthusiastic.

"It would be terrific to have you as part of the team," he said. "You'd bring a background in theater, acting, psychology, human motivation, all of which we are sorely lacking. And, you'd be able to connect us with people throughout the entertainment industry," he added.

I was dumbfounded, ecstatic, and terrified.

Here was a renowned computer scientist echoing the excitement of my new colleague, Scott Stevens. These computer scientists were more open to interdisciplinary cooperation, more visionary than my own colleagues in drama. Pressing my luck, I asked for a raise. The sum I suggested would have been unthinkable in the School of Drama. But since the motivation behind my bold moves was to genuinely change my life, why shouldn't it include making more money as well? Trust me when I say I never thought I'd manage to make a life-changing career move and improve myself financially, but that's exactly what happened. Not only had the door been opened, but I was being carried over the threshold, too.

My next task was to inform my department head, Elisabeth Orion, of my desire to step down as Associate Head. This was painful because Lis, as we all called her, had been a magnificent colleague and leader, as devoted to the students as any teacher I had met before or have encountered since. She had always treated me with kindness and respect, and together we made a formidable team. A classically trained actress whose entire life had been the stage, she personified acting as a vocation and not just a profession. Everyone associated with Carnegie Mellon Drama believed that acting required as much spiritual devotion as entering a religious order. I was about to leave the abbey.

I embraced then—and continue to embrace—the maxim that the only constant in life is change. So, after devoting fifteen years of my life to the School of Drama, intent on devoting myself to the future I envisioned, I resigned as Associate Head and remained on the faculty just to teach a few classes. I knew it might prove a lonely journey at first. I thought back to the 1966 premiere of *Star Trek*. As an eager thirteen-year-old caught up in the "space race," whose leisure reading consisted mainly of science-fiction pulp, I was captivated by the series right from its opening narration, with its exhortation to "boldly go where no man has gone before." The word that stood out then, and came back to me as I contemplated my new life, was "boldly." That, and an old beer commercial proclaiming, "Go for the gusto or don't go at all," were my mantras as I dove headlong into my new pursuit.

Chapter Two
In the Beginning

I immediately immersed myself in the Informedia Project, wanting to learn as much as I could about this exciting technology and trying desperately to overcome lingering fears of inadequacy in this new field. With my background in theater, I felt quite comfortable talking about all aspects of the art form; even though my doctorate was in theater history, literature, and criticism, I knew I was a more-than-competent actor, had directed a number of productions, and was an accomplished voice-over talent. Theater was my bailiwick. But what aptitude did I bring to the technological aspect of digital entertainment?

During Informedia team meetings, the conversation inevitably turned to the technical details of programming, functionality, database management, servers, and myriad other things that seemed complex, at least to me. Try as I might to remain as tuned-in as possible, the tape loop in my head kept repeating, *What are they talking about? Am I supposed to understand this? I feel like a complete idiot.* If I waited long enough, the conversation would usually return to the actual uses and applications of the technology. That was where I could contribute and feel at ease. Increasingly, though, I began to wonder why I couldn't gain knowledge of the technical aspects of our discussions.

These meetings provoked in me a fervent desire to learn. It seemed too easy to dismiss the conversation as techno-speak or completely beyond my intellectual abilities. Something told me that even though it would never be a primary skill of mine, understanding the technical side of Informedia could only make me a better team member. At that point, it was only a gut reaction. The realization that artists and technicians really do think alike had not yet germinated.

Informedia didn't just spring up out of nowhere at Carnegie Mellon—it possessed a thoroughbred pedigree. The very concept of a searchable digital media database system grew out of a search engine developed by Dr. Michael L. "Fuzzy" Mauldin and a team of researchers at the university's Center for Machine Translation. First launched in 1994, it was given the name Lycos, from the Latin name for the predatory wolf spider. Sensing the commercial possibilities of this search engine in the rapidly developing Internet age, Fuzzy approached the Technology Transfer Office about the idea of spinning it off as a company. It turned out to be the right idea at the right time.

I arrived at Informedia at a time when shoptalk often focused on the fortune Fuzzy would make when Lycos had its initial public stock offering (IPO). At the time I didn't even know what that meant. These conjectures proved true. In 1996, Lycos executed the fastest IPO from inception to offering in NASDAQ history. Its meteoric rise continued into 1997, when it became one of the first profitable Internet businesses in the world. By 1999, Lycos was by its own account the most visited website in the world, with a presence in more than forty countries. None of these business milestones, or the vast wealth accumulated by our former colleague, was lost on the remaining members of Informedia. We were witnessing the dot-com boom from the sidelines, and even I took note of what was happening.

Shortly after Fuzzy Mauldin went off to make Internet history, Scott Stevens approached me with an entrepreneurial idea tied to yet another aspect of the Informedia technology: synthetic interviews. Synthetic interviews were conceived and developed by Scott Stevens and Michael Christel, my new colleagues. They provided a means of conversing in-depth with a video image, permitting users to ask questions in a conversational manner, just as they would in a real-world, face-to-face encounter. The user would receive relevant, pertinent answers to the questions he or she asked. Synthetic interviews were accessible via either typed or spoken interfaces, the latter using the Sphinx speech recognition technology developed at Carnegie Mellon's Language Technology Institute.

In the course of a synthetic interview, a user could discover a character's behavior, likes and dislikes, values, qualities, influences, beliefs, and other personal knowledge; it created a kind of computer-generated interpersonal relationship. The synthetic interview also attempted to capture and convey the core human attributes of reflection, humor, perplexity, bewilderment, frustration, and enjoyment; in that way, it created nothing less than a "dyad"—a socially significant relationship forged from an interchange between two individuals, one human and the other computer-generated or video-captured.

The potential of the synthetic interview ignited my personal fervor because of its inherent dramatic qualities. I immediately envisioned countless applications for this technology, and saw a way to contribute my theatrical skills to the effort.

In addition to spending as much time as possible in the Informedia lab, I all but actually moved into Scott's computer science office. I guess I was counting on the power of osmosis; that is, if I hung around long enough, listening to his conversations with students, colleagues, and other researchers, some of his knowledge—and the reasoning behind it—might rub off on me. It was a little bit like learning a foreign language through total immersion. If I heard a term I didn't understand (which was just about every other word in the early years), I could ask him to explain it. Unfortunately for Scott, I often asked for the same explanation multiple times. But gradually, some of this new language actually began to sink in.

One morning, I walked into Scott's office only to be whisked out again. Scott was more than in a hurry; urgency was in the air. "Where are we going?" I asked, out of breath.

"We have a meeting with Raj," Scott declared. My life was about to change yet again, this time as a result of an otherworldly encounter with the Dean of the School of Computer Science, Raj Reddy.

Now, a meeting with Raj could generate fear and trembling in even a seasoned department veteran. Raj is a living legend within the realms of computer science, artificial intelligence, and most definitely "real" intelligence. Before coming to Carnegie Mellon, he served on the faculty of Stanford, where he was the founding director of the Robotics Institute and dean of the School of Computer Science. He is a recipient of the Turing Award, the computer science equivalent of the Nobel Prize. Brilliance can be intimidating, and Raj had the art of intimidation down to a science. I shared Scott's anxiety as we approached Raj's office. He was waiting for us. Clearly, the matter was urgent.

Before we had settled ourselves in our chairs, he began speaking in a calm yet incisive voice. "I would like to make a splash at the upcoming ACM [Association for Computing Machinery] Conference in San Jose—so I would like you to do something spectacular using the synthetic interview technology," Raj told us. I was already lost, trying to figure out what ACM might stand for.

"Like what?" Scott inquired.

"Well," Raj said, "I'd like you to bring someone back from the dead."

Huh? Did this world-famous scientist just say what I thought he said? Before I could contemplate the matter further, Scott replied rather nonchalantly, "Ah, yes. Hmm. Sure. Bring someone back from the dead? I think we could do that. How much time would we have?"

"Would three months be long enough?"

"Oh, three months. Well, yes, yes, I think so," Scott concluded.

The meeting was over. We were ushered out of Raj's office contemplating our mission. After a minute of silence, I stopped dead in my tracks and said incredulously, "Scott, what just happened back there?" He gave me a quizzical look, as if it were all so obvious he wondered why I was asking.

"What do you mean?" he replied.

"What do I mean?! Unless I had a stroke and everything got garbled, I thought Raj just asked us to bring someone back from the dead."

"Well, yes, what about it?"

"Well, how exactly are we going to do that? I mean can you guys do that? I figured you all were smart but that would be a pretty nifty trick for sure."

Scott sighed and shook his head. He probably never imagined that working with a technologically inept drama professor would be so trying. "Of course we aren't *really* going to bring someone back from the dead," he assured me, like

Abbott consoling Costello. "That would be a little hard. But we can make it appear that way."

I've always liked the verb "appear," since theater is all about appearances—as in illusion, make-believe, mimicry, and fantasy. "How?" I inquired eagerly.

"Simple. Synthetic interviews."

Suddenly, I not only got it but also found myself very excited, champing at the bit. The mental wheels were spinning. My enthusiasm ratcheted up even more when I realized we would have an audience for this feat, just like in the theater. We faced the prospect of creating an interactive experience that would be seen by the best and brightest minds in all computer science—and to pull it off would require the core skills of theater professionals. I was elated. My purpose in computer science was becoming clearer.

The first thing Scott and I had to do was decide on the character who would be the subject of the synthetic interview. I knew the technology was still far from perfect. In fact, it had a noticeable error rate, those times when the computer-generated "interviewee" gave an incorrect or irrelevant answer. This error rate was a genuine cause for concern, especially when the Sphinx speech recognition software (then still in its infancy) was used as the interface to the video database.

It became essential to find a character that would make for an entertaining and engaging interaction—even when the wrong answer to a question was called up by the system. So, the casting question became: Who can give you a wrong answer to a serious question but still leave you feeling you got your money's worth? The answer was simple: a genius!

Since the genius category isn't all that large, things narrowed down pretty quickly. I recalled an amazing stage performance I had seen years earlier called "You Know Al, He's a Funny Guy," a one-man show by a talented character actor named Jerry Maher, who portrayed the world-famous Nobel Prize—winning physicist Albert Einstein. Einstein would be our genius! I had found Jerry's portrayal of Einstein so compelling and instructive that a few years earlier I had invited him to perform at freshman orientation for engineering students. When I contacted him about making a synthetic interview he didn't exactly know what I was talking about, but he instantly comprehended the most important thing: It's a job!

The challenge we set for ourselves was to actually create a *willing suspension of disbelief* on the part of the user, the ultimate goal of most performances done in the realistic style. The idea is to get the audience to set aside what they know to be true (that is, the fact that they are sitting in a theater watching a performance) and really believe, at least for a little while, in the reality of what is occurring on stage. In this way, viewers can enter into the experience of the play, feeling empathy, sympathy, pity, joy, laughter, anger, and myriad other human emotions right along with the characters. Scott and I wanted to create this same theatrical alchemy in the "interviewer," making him or her believe in the conversation taking place. The challenge was whether we could achieve that with a technology-mediated performance.

Since Einstein was long dead, we toyed with how to make his reappearance in some way plausible. We decided to have him float against a backdrop of stars, a kind of eternal figure. Users would be communicating with him amidst the vast ether of space. Perfect—we could dispense with a set, thus saving a few dollars and lots of time. We opted for a "talking head" format, shooting Jerry from the waist up so as not to create a Wizard of Oz–style floating head. We wouldn't want to scare any Cowardly Lions, after all!

Over the course of a week, we videotaped Jerry sitting in a chair against a blue screen. We settled on a specific posture from which Jerry commenced and concluded each answer, to indicate when his response was complete. In post-production, we swapped out the blue background for a black galactic star field and applied a gradual fade to Jerry's torso so that when his image was presented using a 3-D holographic projector, users would see Einstein floating amidst the cosmic ether. To our delight, the effect worked well.

The decision to go with a character who would sound brilliant even when providing the "wrong" answer was our own stroke of genius. As I mentioned, Sphinx was a delicate technology at that time. Depending upon the tone, timbre, and pronunciation of the user, rather strange interpretations and misreading of the questions could take place, resulting in some truly bizarre responses. The key was to make the erroneous response an enjoyable—even enlightening—experience. To that end, we created a large default library from which Einstein could draw in replying to questions outside the "domain knowledge" we'd created for him. Despite Synthetic Einstein's exhaustive knowledge base, curve balls came along quite often. "What time is it?" was a very popular question. And the default library was no help when the system believed it heard a question that existed within the database.

One day, an excited guest tester asked Einstein the meaning of life. That question existed within the database; the real Einstein had been asked it on numerous occasions and had always given pithy, insightful, and dramatic responses, all of which were at Synthetic Einstein's disposal. In this instance, however, who knows what Sphinx "heard," because Einstein gave the answer to the question, "Why don't you wear socks?"

User: What is the meaning of life?

Einstein: When I was young I found that the big toe always made a hole in the sock. So I stopped wearing socks.

I was standing off to the side at the time holding my head in my hands, remembering the painful times I'd watched an actor forget a line or give the wrong cue. To my utter amazement, I heard the guest declare, "Yes, I get it. Life is like a sock, confining, stifling the urge to live, choking off one's creativity, stretching around us like a straitjacket of confinement and restraint. So, we must act like the big toe, breaking out of that confinement, shedding the constraints keeping us bottled up in a meaningless existence. Oh, thank you Dr. Einstein, thank you!" That person went skipping off into the conference biomass with the widest smile I had ever seen on a geek.

I knew then and there that we were onto something big—and the feeling was confirmed when Scott and I noticed one of the convention center sanitation workers bringing a coworker over to introduce him to his "friend" Al.

The worldwide attention garnered by the synthetic interview technology led Scott, Mike, Alex Hauptmann (our speech recognition expert), and I to create Grand Illusion Studios, my first involvement in a spin-off company. We sought to adapt the technology to a variety of entertainment and education purposes. These early explorations validated my belief that computer scientists and dramatists could indeed work together in the creation of new forms of digital entertainment and education. It turned out that the Einstein project was just the first of many exciting and amazing things I'd be involved in.

Unfortunately, it would turn out that we gave our company a name that was all too apt. Grand Illusion Studios was acquired in the midst of the dot-com boom. For a precious few months, we were all dot-com millionaires besieged by friends we never knew we had. I was approached for endowed chairs, naming rights, venture capital funding—all manner of philanthropic opportunity. I was amazed at the ease with which technology was being embraced and purchased by folks with minimal technological acumen.

As quickly as we had become millionaires is as quickly as it all disappeared. We sort of knew something was amiss when the CEO of the company that had acquired Grand Illusion was arrested for fraud and carted off to jail. We might be professors, but we were smart enough to know we—and the university— had been had. In many ways it was a relief to go back to being a middle-class "pauper" after having lived the life—even if it was just for a short time—of a dot-com entrepreneurial prince.

While I was absorbed in my adventures with Einstein, Raj Reddy was serving on an advisory committee for the University of Southern California, investigating the impending digitization of the motion picture industry. Raj realized this transformation was nothing less than a paradigm shift. When he returned to Pittsburgh, it occurred to him that Carnegie Mellon was well suited—maybe even better suited than USC—to move into the digital arts arena. After all, we had a world-class computer science school as well as the first degree-granting drama program in the world, boasting so many alumni in the entertainment industry that they were referred to as the Hollywood and Broadway mafia.

One day in 1996, Raj called Scott and me back into his office. He had had another daring idea. I figured since bringing someone back from the dead had proved so much easier than I had feared, we would certainly succeed at whatever challenge he conjured up for us this time. Instead of any specific task, however, Raj talked to us about USC's decision to establish an Entertainment Technology Center. He then asked Scott and me to consider establishing a similar initiative at Carnegie Mellon. There would be no fixed timetable and no funding. As broad and simple as that. We walked away from the meeting pondering what an ETC would look like and who could be tapped to become part of such an initiative at Carnegie Mellon.

I believe firmly in tuning in to the zeitgeist (literally, "the spirit of the age"). As it turns out, it was not only Raj who was drawn to the technological sea change occurring in the motion picture industry. So were many members of the aforementioned Carnegie Mellon Hollywood mafia. In an example of true serendipity, the members of the School of Drama Advisory Committee were returning to campus to conduct their biennial board meeting. They would compile a list of recommendations and present these to the new university president, Jared Cohon. In 1997, these events would converge in startling fashion.

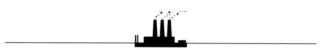

What I learned during this period was the importance of being attuned to more than just one's personal desires and ambitions. If you truly believe the answer is blowing in the wind, then you need to go outside to feel it. I stepped outside my previous existence and, in doing so, discovered an alluring vortex. This funnel-cloud of creativity would soon develop into a veritable tornado of innovation.

Chapter Three

Close Encounters of the Academic Kind

Scott Stevens and I embraced Raj's charge to contemplate what an Entertainment Technology Center might look like, wondering whether it should be a degree-granting academic program or a pure research institute like the one at the University of Southern California. At the same time, unbeknownst to me, another computer science professor was engaged in a parallel development. His name was Randy Pausch.

Randy had studied computer science at Brown, earning his undergraduate degree in 1982. In 1988, he got his Ph.D. in computer science from Carnegie Mellon.

Randy was hired immediately as an assistant professor of computer science at the University of Virginia's School of Engineering and Applied Science. In 1997, the same year Scott Stevens and I teamed up to work on synthetic interviews at CMU, and through our spin-off company, Grand Illusion Studios, Jim Morris, then-head of the Computer Science Department at Carnegie Mellon, lured Randy back with a promise that he could bring his entire Stage 3 research laboratory from the University of Virginia. Jim made Randy a tenured associate professor of computer science, human-computer interaction, and design, and gave him a free hand in developing innovative courses. The prodigal son had returned home. I had no idea who he was, though we were essentially cohabitating in the School of Computer Science, and with shared interests, no less.

There would also be a homecoming of sorts that year for a collection of Drama alumni who comprised the School of Drama Advisory Board. The Advisory Board had been established by former Carnegie Mellon President Robert Mehrabian as a clever way to encourage regular visits by successful alumni. These working alumni were in touch with the latest trends and opportunities in Hollywood, New York, and elsewhere, and the purpose of the Board was to help make sure that the school was teaching courses relevant to the evolving needs of theater, film, and television.

During the 1997 visit by the Drama Advisory Board, a great deal of time and energy was spent discussing the paradigm shift occurring in the entertainment industry. Hollywood, they felt, was in the midst of a production realignment triggered by the introduction of computers and fueled by the rapid digitization of all facets of the creative process. These industry giants recognized this convergence of art and technology as a real step forward, with the twin benefits of reduced production costs (after an initial ramp-up period) and a pending explosion of new kinds of creative content.

At the same time, over in computer science, Randy Pausch was establishing a new course that was attracting a great deal of attention among students and faculty alike. A course he developed called "Building Virtual Worlds" was the first to be cross-listed by every department within the College of Fine Arts as well as the School of Computer Science. It would be the first course to fully embrace interactive digital media in a practical, hands-on manner. Randy recruited students from all majors into his unique interdisciplinary experiment; his "virtual worlds" were to include every facet of such: the software, the art assets, the interface, the modes of interaction, the story, the characters, and the unique experience of inhabiting a virtual environment.

This course so resonated with young people that Randy was deluged with applicants. He insisted on interviewing each one personally, reviewing portfolios, examining code samples, and ascertaining each candidate's interest in virtual reality. A prior sabbatical at Disney had convinced him that a good computer science education had to include teamwork exercises, so he also assessed each student's willingness to work in teams.

I was unaware that any of this was occurring in my own backyard. The Drama Advisory Board presented its report to Carnegie Mellon president, Jared

Cohon and then-provost, Paul Christiano, with the recommendation that Carnegie Mellon embrace the digital revolution. As a result, Drs. Cohon and Christiano decided to create an internal committee charged with investigating how the university could embrace these new realities.

I was asked by the provost to be on this committee, which came as no surprise as the success of the synthetic interview technology, the international press it had garnered, and the resulting spin-off company were on the university's radar screen. These were the heady days of the dot-com era when university administrators saw dollar signs embedded in every new technological venture. Establishing academic programs in digital interactive media seemed to make a great deal of sense. The devil would be in the details.

In the early meetings, I made a point of talking about the Entertainment Technology Center that Raj Reddy had asked Scott Stevens and me to think about establishing, well before the Drama Advisory Board visited campus. I stressed that perhaps computer science had already taken that important first step and the rest of the university was just catching up. It was an arrogant posture, but I am very human.

I am not a good committee member. Frankly, I loathe committees. I have always believed that committees are what you blame when the decisions made by a majority don't work out. I am acutely aware of my deleterious presence on a committee, so, for the most part, I try to shut up and listen to the debate.

Sometimes, though, even silence doesn't work for me. In high school I was removed from a social studies class once because of my negative presence— even though I seldom said anything and actually enjoyed the teacher and subject. When the teacher called me aside to inform me I was no longer her student and had been reassigned to another section, I asked why.

"Because you are a disruption," she declared rather matter-of-factly.

"How can I be a disruption," I protested. "I never say anything in class. I always pay attention. I like the class."

"But you *look*. Whenever someone says something you disagree with or find fault with, you turn and look at them. I don't know what vibe you are sending out when you do that, but it's enough to make them never want to say anything in class again."

Keeping my past in mind, I tried to make my rare statements to the committee as salient, pertinent, and enlightening as possible. I also tried to make my comments declarative and succinct. I refrained from giving the *look* unless it was absolutely necessary.

One person on the committee who spoke a great deal was Randy Pausch. He made a strong impression on me, but I wasn't sure if that was good or bad. Physically, he reminded me of a tall, dark, and handsome Beach Boy, though he hailed from Baltimore, Maryland. Or, he could have been a preppie from central casting, and I don't mean that negatively. I was in no way surprised to discover he had been a star athlete in high school. I found myself observing and listening to him very intently. He emanated the persona of an accomplished researcher even though I really didn't understand what virtual reality was at the time.

What distinguished Randy from all the other computer scientists on the committee was his palpable and contagious enthusiasm. I could tell at once this was someone perennially in search of knowledge and its potential applicability. He seemed a practical researcher in the same vein as my Informedia colleague Scott Stevens. Randy seemed to share my belief that nothing is more elegant than a working application of technology. If you could demonstrate tangibly the way any technology might benefit humankind, you would be providing an educational experience second to none. Randy's impassioned contributions to the ETC discussions, along with the growing excitement he was generating with his Building Virtual Worlds course, continued to impress and inspire me.

The question of who should lead the ETC was becoming a front-burner issue. I knew I desperately wanted the chance to take on a leading role. I do not recall the exact moment when the idea of codirectors for the Entertainment Technology Center was posited, but am fairly certain it was the suggestion of Provost Paul Christiano. The reasoning was solid even then. This new field of entertainment technology was much broader than any one individual could grasp, save perhaps for a few geniuses like Steven Jobs or Pixar's John Lasseter or Ed Catmull—and they weren't likely to move to Pittsburgh. So it seemed logical to bring together a computer scientist with a real desire to reach across the technological divide separating the arts and sciences, and a drama professor who had boldly gone where no one like him had gone before. I knew that if leadership was going to be split in this way, I was the logical choice to represent the College of Fine Arts.

"Entertainment" could exist on its own, as it had for millennia, but the "technology" part of the title would require very specific skill sets and expertise that I did not possess at the time. I was smart enough to know that any program with the words "entertainment" and "technology" in its title needed to be balanced. It required a serious technology component in order to fulfill its mission of bringing right-brain and left-brain students together in a novel way. Randy Pausch was the logical choice to represent the left brain.

As it looked ever more likely that Randy would be the designated representative from the School of Computer Science, I decided it was time to learn as much about him as I could. So I asked him if I could visit his Stage 3 laboratory in Wean Hall. Randy agreed right away and a visit was arranged.

Instead of a traditional, drab laboratory, the Stage 3 lab more closely resembled a toy store. The space was awash with color and filled with toys, games, and stuffed animals—lots of stuffed animals, some hanging from the ceiling. Randy had wisely banished the use of fluorescent lights, so the colorful stuffed animals were illuminated by incandescent lamps. The theme was clearly one of fun, comfort, and contentedness. As a theater person, I felt right at home, but was amazed by it all. This was the School of Computer Science, deep inside a Berlin bunker of a building. Clearly, Randy intended his lab to inspire creativity and out-of-the-box thinking. The Stage 3 students were extremely dedicated, clearly having fun and learning simultaneously, and what they were doing was fascinating.

Then I was introduced to Alice.

Alice began as a piece of rapid 3-D prototyping software that could be used in the creation of storyboards. (Storyboards are pictorial series of hand-drawings, illustrations, sketches, or images displayed in temporal sequence—like a comic strip. They are used to help visualize sequential action.) While storyboarding was created by the Walt Disney Company to preview its animated shorts, the process has been adapted to all kinds of entertainment media. As anyone who has ever crafted a storyboard knows, the process can be a tedious and intricate operation. Randy recognized that a digital 3-D storyboarding tool could be a major technological benefit to the movie industry. What's more, the technology could be adapted for use by theme parks and other location-based entertainment venues, where sequential actions, encounters, and settings create meaningful experiences.

Other companies had recognized this need as well. Before long, commercial tools had been created that addressed this industry need. Alice's original objective was soon eclipsed. Rather than allow this significant research to go to waste, Randy and his team focused on its tremendous potential for teaching the fundamentals of programming to students.

A review of the Alice software reveals many of Randy Pausch's core pedagogic and personal philosophies. First, Randy insisted that Alice be free and open-source. Second, he made sure it would run on Microsoft Windows, Mac, and Linux platforms, to provide maximum usability. And third, he targeted a demographic that had been underserved in the area of computer science: middle-school–age *female* students.

As Randy set about transforming Alice into a teaching program, he was careful to transcend his left-brain orientation. He knew that the true appeal for that particular age group would be in what could be accomplished with the programming, rather than the programming process itself. He settled on storytelling.

Randy and his Stage 3 team created a software program that has been proven in clinical studies to raise the grades of students in introductory programming classes while simultaneously increasing the retention rate of students in computer science. Why? Because Randy and his team made computer programming an intrinsically fun experience with an immediate payoff. In theatrical terms, Randy focused on the *motivations* for pursuing study in computer programming. Alice transcended its intellectual and mathematical means to attract users to its ends.

Acquainting myself with the Stage 3 group and its work on Alice proved an important step in coming to understand Randy's academic research and personal charisma. He was a Pied Piper of computer science. Faculty members at research universities usually oversee graduate students who do the actual research, analysis, data compilation, and publication. It is a kind of academic rite of passage that often fosters questionable, ambiguous relationships between the "principal investigator" and his or her minions. I saw none of that in Randy's Stage 3 lab. What I did see was a genuine team, striving to achieve a common goal. They were all true believers and happy to be such. It reminded me very much of the camaraderie among a cast of actors as they transform into a true ensemble.

Shortly thereafter, I discovered Randy's penchant for performance. It was manifest in the end-of-semester public presentation of the "worlds" created in his Building Virtual Worlds class. The "BVW show," a public presentation of the student teams' best work, takes place each year during the first week of December. I approached my first show not knowing what to expect, but with the same receptiveness I bring to any live performance.

The show was presented in the five hundred–seat McConomy Auditorium, an adequate lecture theater, but by no means a true performance venue. What struck me immediately, though, was the serpentine line of excited students eager for entry. I like lines of people queuing up to see live performance. In fact, I dream of it! The buzz was palpable, the excitement genuine. My curiosity was definitely piqued.

One aspect of the Building Virtual Worlds show that had a tremendous impact on me and provided insight into the psyche of my soon-to-be partner was the conferring of the First Penguin Award, given with great fanfare by Randy to that group of students who took the biggest gamble in terms of ideas and technology but failed to achieve their stated goal. It was in essence a "glorious failure" award, offering positive reinforcement for out-of-the-box thinking, team aspiration, and imaginative daring.

Randy was excited and proud to announce the Penguin Award recipients and to describe their failed endeavor. This struck me as odd at first. In theater, we use the rehearsal period to take risks. We are encouraged to explore character and plot from as many different angles as possible. We are taught to bring myriad ideas to the rehearsal, knowing it is always easier to pull back, cut down, and restrain than it is to add to characterization. But when it is time for the show to open, the performance is pretty much locked down. Any new revelations from that point on are discussed with the director, stage manager, and other cast members. It would be unthinkable for us to reward an actor who had a terrific idea that he failed to realize. Yet here was a professor recognizing students for their failures. It was only later that I comprehended the brilliance of this approach.

As the designated students assembled on the stage of McConomy Auditorium to receive the First Penguin Award, there were smiles, but no overt hoopla or boisterousness. Randy proceeded to inform the audience of the wild idea the team attempted to realize, stressing its innate innovation, how it attempted to push technology to do things it wasn't originally designed to achieve, and how the team struggled to achieve this objective, albeit for naught. Randy then handed each team member a certificate and a small stuffed penguin—in keeping with his penchant for stuffed animals.

The First Penguin Award has now become a staple of the BVW class and is a tangible manifestation of Randy's belief that brick walls (obstacles) serve only to help you gauge the seriousness of your aspiration. Over the years, a mystique has grown up around it. It is seen as a badge of honor, though it remains secondary to creating a successful project. First Penguin Award recipients are recognized during the BVW Show, but their world isn't presented. I think if you were to ask any ETC student whether they'd prefer to win the First Penguin Award or have their team's work selected for inclusion in the show, the latter would win in a landslide.

Step by step, I came to see the brilliance and daring of Randy's approach. Most academics agree that school is one of the few places where one is encouraged to reach for the stars. What Randy believed is that in doing so, failure should be an honorable result. I question whether most of us in education nowadays actually support that contention. The First Penguin Award is a tangible expression of Randy's philosophy. I am honored to say that in the Entertainment Technology Center we continue to live up to it.

After seeing the Alice work going on in Randy's Stage 3 lab and the interactive virtual reality performances of his Building Virtual Worlds show, I came to share his vision. Both of these initiatives were born of his instinctive understanding that learning and entertainment truly enhance each other. In this regard, Randy shared the mindset and philosophy of one of his heroes: Marshall McLuhan. The McLuhan maxim that Randy recited every chance he could, and that became a de facto motto of the ETC, was: "Anyone who thinks there is a difference between education and entertainment doesn't know much about either."

Randy had crafted software, a curriculum, and a physical environment that were truly complementary. His work was all about building things, not just talking about them. I had found my supreme kindred spirit in computer science. Perhaps we really had a lot more in common than we had been led to believe by the purveyors of distinction and separation. Instead of being a stranger in a strange land, I was starting to feel very much at home.

Chapter Four
If We Build It,
Will They Come?

As it looked more likely that Randy and I would team up to lead the Entertainment Technology Center, there were whispered warnings around campus of imminent disaster approaching. The two of us were perceived as alpha males, powerful individuals, comfortable with being in charge. We were seen as leaders whom others willingly followed, doers, movers-and-shakers. The news that we'd be working together had colleagues placing bets on which one of us would be found floating face down in one of Pittsburgh's three rivers. It was presumed that either Randy's arrogance or my temper would surely do in one of us.

Fortunately, Randy and I also quickly became aware of the potential for discord. What became apparent to both of us as we got to know each other was that while we were alpha males, we were from vastly different cultures. The battle for domination was essentially neutralized when we realized it wasn't about which lion would rule the pride, because we were actually two distinctive breeds sharing the same enclosure. And that environment was unfamiliar to both of us—since neither Randy nor I were hardcore video game players, and video games were the primary manifestation of interactivity at that time. What our colleagues overlooked was that there is precedence in nature for alpha male coalitions, where two or more dominant individuals share leadership of the herd to ensure the safety and survival of the group. I guess you could say that Randy and I were motivated by the safety and survival of ourselves.

Randy and I both knew that we personified the right-brain/left-brain dichotomy:

RIGHT BRAIN	LEFT BRAIN
Random	Logical sequential
Approximate calculation	Exact computation
Intuitive	Rational
Synthesizing	Analytical
Subjective	Objective
Prosodic	Verbal, symbolic, and mathematical facility
Holistic processing	Linear compositing of information
Fantasy-oriented	Reality-based

Randy and I fit these classifications about as perfectly as any pair I have ever met: I'm a classic right-brain type, and he held down the left. Despite our seemingly glaring differences, however, we were united in our wholehearted belief in individual responsibility. We viewed the right-brain/left-brain divide as a matter of personal choice, as opting to take on specific roles for reasons more psychological than organic. And if these behaviors are, to a large degree, learned, they can also be modified. We also knew that our success would depend on how well we bridged this divide. If we could create a place where artists and technologists could feel equally at home, a place where they would learn to respect and admire each other and work together in holistic endeavors, then we would be doing a service to education in America.

Along with our reflections on the right-brain/left-brain divide, Randy and I pondered the timing of the creation of the ETC in light of the evolving technological revolution. From the founding in 1998 through today, people have commended and complimented us on being so visionary. Oddly enough, Randy and I always viewed its creation as a *reactionary* event. We weren't leading so much as following. *Who* we were following, however, turned out to be what was really revolutionary about the center. We were following in the footsteps of our *students*.

One of the first decisions we had to make was what we would call the degree we intended to grant. Randy and I were in agreement that what we called this degree would set the tone for the entire curriculum. We agreed that the course of study should be professional in nature. We wanted our students to graduate directly into the entertainment technology industry—or to possess the knowledge, wherewithal, and drive to create entirely new industries.

That prompted an interesting question that Randy and I had to deal with immediately. Should we, in fact, become the "Video Game Center" and eschew the Entertainment Technology name to which I had grown so committed? After some discussion we agreed that we didn't feel comfortable heading up a video game center because we weren't hardcore gamers. More important, though, was our shared view that technology-mediated interactivity was the variable that was changing the field of entertainment. Focusing solely on video games would undoubtedly become a limiting factor as new technologies proliferated and infiltrated all aspects of society. We were also of the shared belief that no matter what activity (work or play) one engaged in, there should be a palpable level of fun, entertainment, pleasure, release, and transformation associated with it. We wanted to build our program on the broadest definition of entertainment that we could devise. Video games would most definitely be a fundamental part of the ETC, but not its exclusive enterprise.

So . . . back to the question of what to call the degree we would offer. Traditional Masters programs confer Master of Art (M.A.) or Master of Science (M.S.) degrees. These programs tend to focus on scholarly, academic, or critical study within a given field. The degrees are seen as steps toward a Doctoral degree (Ph.D.). The Master of Fine Arts degree (M.F.A.), on the other hand, focuses on practice in a particular field of artistic endeavor. It is considered a terminal degree, the highest level of academic accomplishment for a professional discipline.

We opted for the designation Master of Entertainment Technology (M.E.T.). It would be a one-of-a-kind, specialized degree program embracing the interdisciplinary field of entertainment technology. We hoped it might become a model for others.

Randy and I next set about crafting a curriculum. It wasn't long before we realized that we were approaching this in an all-too-traditional way, cramming as many courses as possible into a finite amount of time. We found ourselves looking at a jam-packed semester, busily counting credit hours. Our radical new program was starting to look traditional. Something just wasn't right.

This uneasy feeling was exacerbated when we had our first meetings with the college councils of both the College of Fine Arts and the School of Computer Science, the academic governing bodies of each college. Discussion quickly spiraled into competing content and unit-hour demands from each college, even though the council members knew even less about entertainment technology than we did. The entire exercise left a bad taste in our mouths. It also fueled a desire to fight fire with fire.

One day we were sitting in Randy's office, my new home away from home since the School of Computer Science had no vacant offices. (Randy shared Scott's belief that it was better for the two of us to share an office anyway, to promote osmosis and shared learning.)

We stared at the white board, which was scribbled all over with possible semester schedules and curriculums. There was a lot of sighing going on between the two of us. We then recalled almost simultaneously something Bryan Rogers, then head of the School of Art, had said to us after one exasperating college council meeting. "Why do you even have to have classes?" he said, we presumed, rhetorically. But the thought had taken hold subconsciously.

Randy got up and, to my amazement, erased the classes clogging up the second, third, and fourth semester of studies. "Suppose we didn't require students to do anything other than projects during these terms?" he said.

I smiled with glee. What would once have been considered a radical and potentially outrageous thought suddenly made a whole lot of sense. We looked at a proposed schedule that featured an intensive first semester followed by three semesters of project work, and it all felt right.

"In drama, we expect our students to focus on their mainstage and studio performance work," I added, "But then we burden them with a truckload of classes of dubious value that distract them from their roles. I always thought it would be terrific if students could focus all of their energy on the performance. The schedule we're talking about now, Randy, would be the entertainment technology version of that long-awaited dream. I love it!"

We both felt good about this idea; the first semester curriculum we were proposing was so intense, we labeled it Boot Camp. (As a military veteran, I related well to the concept.) Randy viewed it as Eagle Scout studies on steroids.

This initial immersion semester would consist of four classes. First and foremost would be Randy's Building Virtual Worlds course. This would serve as the foundation class where students would learn as much about teamwork as they would about virtual reality and other input/display technologies.

Another course would be called Visual Story and would be based on the seminal book of the same name by Carnegie Mellon Drama graduate Bruce Block. Bruce recognized early on that the unfolding technology revolution would rely on visual storytelling. Creating harmony and counterpoint between story structure and visual realization would have to become a paramount skill set for our students.

Recognizing the need to understand the structure within a story, I opted to teach a course titled ETC Fundamentals, which would serve multiple purposes. The overarching goal was to convey what I termed the New Poetics—really the "Old" Poetics that Aristotle devised to analyze the structure of tragedy (plot, character, theme, diction, rhythm, spectacle), combined with the elements of interactivity delineated by Janet Murray: immersion, agency, transformation. This course would be augmented by multiple real-world experiences providing tangible examples of story structure in real life.

Rounding out Boot Camp would be a fourth class, Improvisational Acting. Oddly enough, this course generated the most discussion during college council meetings. Within the College of Fine Arts, the question focused on what kind of improvisation acting exercises would be taught. In the School of Computer Science, there was general consternation as to why this course had to be required of all ETC students, especially those with a programming background.

In early 1998, Randy and I went on a tour of West Coast video game, animation, and post-production companies. We traveled around asking studio heads and others what skill sets they would want future employees to possess.

Included in our itinerary was an upstart animation company in San Raphael, California, by the name of Pixar. We met with Ed Catmull, chief technology officer at the time. When we asked him about necessary skill sets, Ed answered without hesitation: "Improvisational acting."

Naturally, that excited me. Even before the tour commenced, I figured Improvisational Acting would be a natural part of the curriculum because it was as close as we come, in real time, to nonlinear storytelling. Ed Catmull, however, offered a different justification.

"It is an anti-ego device," he said matter-of-factly.

This thought intrigued me. "How so?" I inquired.

"In order for improvisational acting to work, you have to be a generous person. If you insist on always having the punch line or getting the laugh, then the entire improv skit falls apart. It only works if the actors have a generosity of spirit. And that is the kind of generosity you need in order to be a successful team player, at least at a place like Pixar."

I had never thought of it from this angle, and found Ed's reasoning brilliant. I recall gently kicking Randy under the table, excited by the synchronicity that existed between what we wanted to do and what someone as renowned as Ed Catmull thought should be part of our curriculum.

During these months of planning, Randy and I got caught up in the excitement about our new venture. But so far, our work was taking place within the confines of the university administration and faculty, along with a few representatives from the industry. We had not yet taken our ideas to potential students. Imagine our surprise, then, when Randy and I showed up at our Wean Hall office one day and found a group of undergraduates waiting for us. In amazement we asked, "Why are you all here?"

Looking like the cast of Luigi Pirandello's famous play *Six Characters in Search of an Author*, the students stated demurely that they had heard "rumors" about Carnegie Mellon establishing something called the Entertainment Technology Center, and that it would offer a new and unique professional degree by the name of Master of Entertainment Technology.

We acknowledged as much, almost as if we had been caught in the act.

"This is something we have been waiting for, dreaming about," they told us, "ever since we got to Carnegie Mellon! Now all of us are either about to graduate or have only a year left in our undergraduate studies. Many of us have even crafted our own self-defined majors, hoping, in effect, to create this very discipline. So, basically, we want to be part of this program!"

Randy and I looked at each other. We told the students truthfully that we really didn't know what we were doing with the degree, that we were essentially making it up as we went along. We just knew that we wanted to create a program that would excite the growing interactive digital media industries and make Carnegie Mellon grads of the program their desired new hires.

They heard us, but revealed no inclination to depart.

We then suggested to them that if they were willing to serve as pioneers—in the truest sense of the word—they would be most welcome to join us in this great experiment.

They took us up on the offer. So, instead of spending more time researching how the program should look and behave, we were joined by eight Carnegie Mellon students who were willing to sustain arrows, floods, droughts, and the veritable unknown to help us create the Master of Entertainment Technology degree program.

It couldn't have been clearer that the ETC was not really leading the evolution of multidisciplinary thought, but was responding to the intellectual sea of change we had sensed but not tangibly grasped. We became a venue for these multidisciplinary folks to have a home and research center, and we advertised and modeled that openness by being codirectors from opposite backgrounds.

This only served to strengthen the original goals of the ETC that we had stated on many occasions:

- Establish world leadership as researchers at the "lunatic fringe of new media content,"
- Produce graduates who pioneer this new content,
- Create a shared culture where technology, fine arts, and other faculty and students mix,

- Impact the emerging commercial market of interactive entertainment, and
- Incubate and spin off companies.

We were very proud of wanting to be on the "lunatic fringe of new media content"—we wanted students who would come up with wild and crazy ideas. All too often, academics claim to want students who "push the envelope" when in fact they don't. Well, we intended to be true to our word, and, for the most part, we've managed it.

A unique policy at Carnegie Mellon that I believe is directly responsible for its proven entrepreneurial spirit is its intellectual property agreement with students. In short, students own any intellectual property they create as members of classes for which they pay tuition and receive academic credit. Since the ETC does not offer scholarships, and because its students receive the vast majority of their academic credit for engaging in projects sponsored by for-profit and not-for-profit institutions, ETC students leave the program owning a great deal of intellectual property of their own creation that is eminently applicable and potentially commercial.

The most exciting and dynamic projects are frequently those pitched by the students. They are a breed apart. They do not know limits. And while sometimes they fall short, when they do hit their mark, the results can be simply amazing. It is these student endeavors that invariably lead to spin-off companies. The ETC has been averaging one spin-off company a year since its creation.

Randy and I insisted that every ETC project have a client, even projects that were student-pitched and undertaken for the pure joy of exploration. Having a client assigned to an ETC project has fundamental pedagogical advantages, too. For instance, odds are pretty high that upon graduation our students will be working in for-profit entertainment companies. Very few of them will have the freedom and financial security to fulfill artistic aspirations without first "paying their dues" in the employ of others. So, we opt to give them the seldom joyous, but always educational, experience of working for a client.

Almost all creative folks (technical and non-technical) develop a love-hate relationship with clients. Clients are like parents: They mean well but they are usually communication-challenged when dealing with young people. Seldom do they speak the same language. For instance, we often have clients who are looking for "cutting-edge technology" and "out-of-the-box thinking." But . . . cutting edge in relation to what? What size box are they hoping we'll think outside of? It is rare indeed for a client and a student team to understand these requests in exactly the same way. What usually happens is that the cutting edge gets dulled into a butter knife while the box in question is seldom bigger than a cereal box.

This obvious recipe for frustration, though, is an important aspect of the ETC education. The challenge becomes: How do you convey creativity, excitement, daring, and risk to a client desirous of change but fearful of failure? If you can learn how to do this, then you have learned an extremely valuable skill no matter where you wind up professionally.

Randy and I always stood by the belief that an ETC project has to be allowed to fail. Now, that doesn't mean we *want* it to fail. We definitely never wanted any project to fail if that failure could be prevented. Failures caused by ignoring the obvious, by neglecting to undertake proper research, by refusing to question one's presumptions, biases, and predilections, or failures caused by refusing to work as a team, while no doubt educational, were considered to be wastes of time and energy. Failure when attempting to devise some new, creative way of achieving a specific goal, however, was completely allowable. In fact, such a failure often proves more beneficial—and more educational—than a success.

In the same way that Pixar's Ed Catmull extolled the virtues of improvisational acting as an anti-ego device, forcing all ETC project teams to work for a client positions the work within the real world of commercial entertainment. Unlike pure art schools, the ETC evaluates the success of an entertainment experience partly by the market's willingness to pay for it. We do not view this as crass commercialism, because we value the content and objective of the experience just as highly. You could say we have a libertarian outlook when it comes to entertainment, since we place the primacy of individual choice and the harsh realities of the marketplace above other more academic concerns.

Randy and I maintained a peaceful and reflective camaraderie within the ETC. Neither of us used our "Dr." titles because we were dealing in a new discipline and learning as much as the students. Frankly, the students were, in most instances, more knowledgeable about specific games and technologies than we were (or perhaps I should just speak for myself!).

When it came to our personal styles, Randy and I clearly manifested our left-brain/right-brain attributes. While we both opted for casual wear as much as possible, Randy was most definitely the preppy member of our dynamic duo. He coordinated. His clothes may not have been immaculately ironed, pressed, or even fashionable, but he definitely fulfilled the image of the dynamic young college professor.

I looked like an aging hippie. I'd happily wear nothing but Hawaiian shirts if I could. My dress was basically random, but always with an eye toward comfort. Not surprisingly, neither of us was inclined toward suits; we viewed them as necessary evils, as costumes. I owned more formal clothes than Randy did, and would periodically opt to dress up as a way of at least trying to make myself look serious. It seldom worked.

The way we spoke and communicated was also stereotypically left brain/right brain. It never ceased to amaze me that Randy responded instantly to emails. Granted, his responses were seldom long or literary gems, but they said what needed to be said. I, on the other hand, took forever to craft a proper response. I wasn't answering email as much as writing scripts, paying attention to spelling, grammar, syntax, tone, objective, and subtext. I tried to make my response worth the wait, but this often resulted in a delay of days or even weeks. Then again, what was time as far as I was concerned?

Not too long after Randy and I teamed up to head the ETC, he invited me to join him in attending a DARPA Conference in Orlando, Florida. DARPA stands for Defense Advanced Research Projects Agency, and is the Department of Defense agency responsible for the development of new technology for use by the military. It is in large part thanks to DARPA that we have the Internet (no offense, Mr. Gore) and the graphical user interface. There were a lot of generals, admirals, distinguished scientists, and assorted other elevated government research folks attending this conference.

I maintained a very low profile throughout, wondering more than once if I hadn't gotten myself into something intellectually way over my head. Out of the blue, during the final general session, the military official serving as host said, "We have had in our midst the past few days a special guest. He is a drama professor who has been working the past few years with computer scientists."

I breathed a sigh of relief. Here I had thought I was the only one to have done such a thing, only to discover that I wasn't alone. I eagerly scanned the room looking for the other wayward artist.

The general continued, "He served as associate head of the famous Carnegie Mellon School of Drama before transferring into computer science to work on the Informedia project."

Egad, he was talking about me! I slunk down into my seat. Thoughts of a very public math exam popped into my head.

"We would like to ask Don Marinelli to stand up. We are eager to hear from him what it has been like for a drama professor to work alongside computer scientists."

Randy led the applause in urging me to stand up. I made my way to the microphone, looked out upon a sea of Ph.D.s, and restated the question: "So, how does it feel to be an artist in the midst of computer scientists?" I paused. I reflected. I dug deep. I fought with myself to utter whatever sounds came closest to the truth.

"I feel right at home," I declared proudly.

Trust me, actors are trained to sense and read audiences, and I could sense their surprise at this statement.

"I mean it," I reiterated. "I feel right at home. This might surprise you, but that's because you may not understand how an artist thinks. I fear many of you believe we go out walking in the woods, lifting our eyes, ears, and arms to heaven, pleading to the muses to strike us with inspiration. And, while that does happen periodically, the truth is that what we teach and practice is a craft. That is why we spell *playwright* with a 'w.' It derives from the same root as, say, *shipwright*—a craftsman of ships.

"As a craft, there are fundamental skills that go into all aspects of dramatic performance. For instance, as a director, I might ask an actor to enter the stage from up left—a traditionally weak area of the stage—cross to center stage to deliver a specific monologue while staring at a spot on the rear wall of the theater just above the audience, then quickly cross to the down right stage area—the most powerful part of the stage. My knowledge of my craft tells me that if the actor does that, then the audience should come to believe, say, that the butler did it."

I saw heads tilt.

"What I have just described is the kind of 'if-then' equation I use within my discipline. It's a kind of algorithm, if you will. So you see, both theater directors and computer scientists engage in cause-and-effect reasoning. The primary difference is that your algorithms are based on mathematics while mine are based on human psychology, language, and literature—making for a much less precise equation. We are, by that measure, brothers and sisters."

Randy and I recognized that the ETC would never be confused with a traditional liberal arts environment or a standard high-technology research institution. We were intent on making it fully hospitable to artists and technologists alike because if you really think about it, they have more things in common than things that separate them. Just like Randy and me.

Chapter Five

Welcome to the Entertainment Technology Center

The experimental emphasis of the ETC grew out of Randy's and my belief that no amount of technology alone can create a compelling experience.

One of the main reasons I gravitated to theater as a young person was that it gave me the ability to become someone else. My conflict-ridden adolescent years provided ample motivation for seeking to transform my existence into a variety of fantasy lives. Theater was indeed an escape for me. Dramatic literature offered a wide range of other worlds, alternative histories, and new families, all filled with intriguing, engaging, curious— and sometimes repugnant—characters that fascinated and excited me. I was considered a very good actor because of my ability to inspire what the English poet Samuel Taylor Coleridge called "the willing suspension of disbelief." I was able to bracket and shelve who I was in "real life" and take on the attributes of someone else. So, it seemed to me that interactive digital media could provide a new way for anyone to free himself and take on the kind of alternative existence that had previously been reserved for actors (or for the insane).

One of the key components of interactive digital media is the *immersion* dynamic. Immersion is the term used to describe the all-encompassing psychological and sensorial experience of a virtual environment.

What always struck me about this technology-mediated dynamic is that we actors have actually been doing this for millennia. Georgia Institute of

Technology professor Janet Murray acknowledges this in her book *Hamlet on the Holodeck* when she states that video game players "are gradually learning to do what actors do, to enact emotionally authentic experiences that we know are not 'real.'"

Randy and I discovered, to our surprise, that most of our students had more varied experiences in *virtual* worlds than in the *corporeal* world. Consequently, the ETC would seek to create technology-mediated experiences that would bridge the dimensional divide between our "real" existence and the virtual world. To do so, however, we would need to make sure our students had a broad-based and shared experiential vocabulary to express what it means to be human. Providing that within a two-year graduate program comprised of students with a variety of language skill levels was a challenge we knew would be hard to meet. But we were determined to try.

Randy and I recognized that the general impression of the video game industry among academics and the mainstream media was less than adulatory. And we agreed with them. From the beginning, we hoped to elevate the nature of video games to a respected art form, laying to rest the current widespread perception of them as, at best, a domestic nuisance and at worst, the cause of sociopathic behavior.

We acknowledged that interactive digital media was, to a large degree, responsible for young people shying away from traditional youthful endeavors. So, Randy and I resolved that one of the underpinnings of the Entertainment Technology Center would be an emphasis on experiencing life and learning in as many forms and varieties as possible.

During my years in Carnegie Mellon Drama, one of the fundamental educational commitments made to the Dramats (our loving term for our students) was to take them to New York City for an annual audition presentation. (This has since been expanded to include Los Angeles.) This showcase of their talent, held before a huge assembly of casting directors, talent agents, managers, directors, and producers, gave the young actors a genuine experience of what show business is like, while simultaneously acquainting them with the hustle and bustle of New York City. And of course the exposure to these professionals could provide fantastic breaks for them. The excursion had become a steadfast part of the students' education, the "icing on the cake" that made matriculating at Carnegie Mellon even more appealing. I figured we needed to do something similar with the ETC.

When I suggested taking the ETC students on what can only be considered a graduate-level "field trip on steroids," Randy became excited by the idea. We debated the merits of taking them to Orlando, where themed entertainment rules, or traveling to Silicon Valley, where video game companies are ubiquitous, or visiting Southern California, where digital animation and post-production companies abound. We decided, ultimately, to take them to as many places as possible—anywhere that promised educational value. The gears were spinning in our heads as we brainstormed possible destinations.

In the midst of one of these discussions, Randy froze, wide-eyed, in one of his characteristic pauses, and exclaimed, "We can stay at KOA!"

Being from Brooklyn, New York, I really didn't understand the reference. I knew what "TKO" meant, likewise "KIA" and "CIA," but "KOA" wasn't ringing any bells.

"What's that?" I asked.

Randy glared and said, "Clearly you were never a Boy Scout!"

How true, how true!

"Kampgrounds of America," he finally explained.

I looked at him like he was deranged. I had, of course, seen those cheery "KOA" signs along the highway, though the corporate misspelling had always bothered me. It was as if the place was designed for illiterates.

"We can all sleep in tents! It will save us money and expose the students to the great outdoors," he said, or something to that effect. I don't recall exactly, because my mind was already going, "Oh no, no, no, no, no; I don't think so; not on your life; over my dead body; lions and tigers and bears, oh my!"

"Are you suggesting we sleep outside?" I stammered.

Randy was bouncing around like Tigger in Winnie the Pooh's Hundred Acre Wood. Clearly, he saw this not only as a bonding experience for everyone, but as actual "fun!"

"Randy," I made clear, "I don't sleep outside. Not even when I was in the Air Force did I have to sleep outside. Why do you think I joined the Air Force in the first place? We had maids at my Reserve Base in Pittsburgh. They don't even have *barracks* in the Air Force—they have *dormitories*. I must insist: If we go on school field trips, then we are going to have to stay in hotels with running water and indoor bathrooms."

I had clearly taken the wind out of Tigger's sails, but I didn't feel too bad about it. I was relieved at having saved myself from being eaten by wolves, or whatever other creatures reside in the wilds of California and Florida.

"Well, okay," Randy countered, clearly deflated by the urban predilections of his codirector. But he quickly rejoined, "If we stay in hotels, though, I have to tell you I only stay at hotels with numbers in their names, like Motel 6 or Super 8."

"Gee," I exclaimed, "What a coincidence! I'm the same way: I really like the Four Seasons!"

Randy's frugality aside, we always stayed at very well-appointed and comfortable hotels, albeit not the Four Seasons. These trips were actually extremely difficult to organize and required quite a bit of stamina. Because ETC students all pay full tuition, we resolved that the trips would be paid for out of their tuition, and that their money would be well spent on truly educational experiences. Spending money on experiential learning became a paramount aspect of the ETC education.

We were similarly careful about spending money on food. Until recently, one of the hallmarks of professional life in Silicon Valley video game and digital media companies was the availability of inexpensive (often free) food and beverages. These companies recognize that their young employees work long hours (often too long) and would benefit from easy access to nutrition. ETC students work long hours, too, in a location without easy access to food. Randy and I decided to make free food available to our ETC students. But, lest they forget that we are a school and not DreamWorks or Google, our menu choices are rather limited. We almost always have ample quantities of ramen noodles and cookies!

It was during one of our early gastronomic discussions that I discovered something about Randy that boded well for our future together. I was contemplating various kinds of instant, frozen, canned, prepackaged, or just-add-water meals with which we could stock the ETC kitchen, while Randy sat quietly. No suggestions were forthcoming. Somewhat exasperated, I demanded, "So tell me, what would you want to eat if you were an ETC student?"

He replied nonchalantly, "I'm not the right person to ask because I always eat the same thing every day for lunch. So it doesn't really matter to me."

"You eat the same thing every day?" I repeated incredulously.

"Yep," he replied proudly, "Turkey on white bread with just a hint of mayonnaise."

I broke out in a wide grin. "You know, Randy," I replied, "The only other person I know who eats the same thing every day for lunch is my wife!" I knew then and there that he and I were going to get along just fine—even if my lunch preferences ran more to a selection of Chinese, Indian, Italian, and Japanese.

Over the years, the ETC has come to call our excursions "field trips" or "adventure modules." When the department was smaller in size, we would ask students to show up bright and early with bags packed for an overnight stay. They would then reach into Randy's precious Mad Hatter's Hat and pull out a colored marble. That marble corresponded to a colored placard attached to a bus idling in the ETC parking lot. Students boarded the buses and were whisked away to a designated location. Team challenges, designed to test their mettle and gauge their ability to come together, awaited them on arrival.

We have found that white-water rafting is a terrific introduction to the rigors of the ETC. If team members do not paddle together, they flip over together. It is as simple as that. And white-water rafting can elicit outright fear in certain individuals, which in turn triggers the instinct in others to help. Tolerance thresholds and many other behavioral indicators manifest themselves. A rope course might bring out the same qualities. Corporations and the military have realized the benefits of "confidence courses" for years; it is about time education caught on to the obvious.

Of course, not everyone has the same definition of experiential learning. I raised more than a few eyebrows within Carnegie Mellon's central administration when I declared ocean cruises to be an essential part of the ETC's experiential curriculum. I raised even more eyebrows when I submitted a healthy five-figure reimbursement receipt!

"A cruise is a field trip?" was the disbelieving response I got from the woman in the accounting office.

"That's a good point," I countered. "It makes more sense to refer to it as field research. You see, a cruise functions as a floating hotel, has multiple-dining experiences, offers different types of restaurant venues, presents Las Vegas—style shows, offers casino gaming, can be considered a nature experience, and, when you think about it, in rough seas is a roller-coaster to boot!"

The silence on the other end of the line indicated that she wasn't buying it.

"Trust me," I reassured her, "every student must write up the experience as an assignment. They also have the option of artistically interpreting it. What has the greatest impact on them, though, is seeing the sun set into the ocean or feeling the strength of the wind the way it blows on the open seas. Others remark that they had never seen the brightness of the stars from the pitch darkness of the open water. It is an amazingly educational experience. Plus, they get a grade for it."

Suffice it to say, the cruise has become an annual event.

The commitment to provide as much active learning as possible came about as a natural extension of Carnegie Mellon's "learn by doing" philosophy, combined with the inherently dynamic nature of the entertainment industry. Because interactive digital media is unique in its ability to create entire virtual universes, it seemed a logical deduction that our students should be exposed to as many different aspects of our own planet as we could fit into two years of study. We needed to weave together technology-mediated experiences with natural wonderment. In other words, we made sure our curriculum combined right-brain art, culture, sports, social, and even culinary experiences, with left-brain technologies that in some way transformed them.

One thing Randy and I began that has become a standard ETC experience is the annual West Coast tour. At the start of each calendar year, the first-year students have made it through Boot Camp and are ready to embark on project work. They must begin to envision working in the digital media and animation industries. To help them get to this point, we take them to the West Coast and arrange for visits to as many video game, location-based entertainment, animation, and post-production companies as possible. We have been blessed with stellar cooperation from companies such as Disney, SONY, Pixar, LucasArts, DreamWorks, Electronic Arts, Activision, Take Two, Shaba, and many more. It's a two-way street, of course: The companies get an early glimpse of the talent that will soon be knocking on their doors, while helping the students figure out which doors they will want to knock on.

The West Coast tour is not limited to potential job-seeking. Always looking for more opportunities to drive home the concept of immersive experience, we try to take a side trip to Muir Woods in Marin County, California. It is safe to assume that today's students have explored vast reaches of the imaginative universe, but very few of them have ever visited a real redwood forest. Taking them to Muir Woods and watching as the giant redwoods remind them just how puny a human can feel within nature is a great thrill. Asking young people to lean against a giant tree and look up, barely able to glimpse blue sky through the foliage canopy, provides them with an experience beyond anything they can glean in a video game.

One of the gifts Randy gave himself after he was diagnosed with pancreatic cancer was a scuba diving trip to the Cayman Islands. Immersion might be the best way of losing oneself in an experience that serves ultimately as a means of finding oneself. Just ask any actor.

On these field trips, Randy and I continually stressed the importance of individual accountability and responsibility, attributes that continually came into play out in the field. Falling short could prove the beginning of an unexpected adventure.

One trip consisted of two buses of ETC students, faculty, and staff driving to Gettysburg, Pennsylvania, to visit the historic (but dated at the time) Civil War Museum. The challenge was to see whether the physical museum adequately captured the historic significance of this important moment in

American history. Students were asked to describe how this location-based venue could be made more meaningful to their generation. What and where could interactivity, augmented reality, and unique input and display devices be used to bring the various artifacts and stories to life?

Our lodging on this trip was at a resort complex not far from Gettysburg. It was the first stop on the road to Norfolk, Virginia, where we would connect the next day with a cruise ship for an overnight cruise-to-nowhere. Punctuality was stressed repeatedly to the students, and always within the context of team responsibility. Bright and early the next morning, we were on our way to Norfolk when one of the students handed me his cell phone.

"What is this?" I asked, surprised.

"Uh, it's for you," he replied demurely. I sensed something interesting was waiting for me on the other end of the line.

"Hi Don," said the voice. I knew immediately it was one of the ETC students. "Hello," I replied very calmly. "Where are you?"

"Uh, I'm back at the resort," came the monotone response. There was a *hint* of remorse, but not enough as far as I was concerned. "And why is that?" I inquired.

"I decided to take a shower," he said.

"Why did you shower so close to our departure time?"

"I don't know," came the reply. "I thought we were leaving at a later time, I guess." Silence. Pause. Pregnant pause. Elephant pregnancy pause . . .

"And what do you expect me to do about this?" I challenged.

"Uh, come back and get me?" he replied hesitantly.

"Well, I'm not going to do that," was my stern reply. I knew every student on the bus was eager to hear how I was going to respond to the situation. I knew exactly what I'd say. This was a graduate program; these students were expected to act as adults. Unfortunately, we discovered that to a large degree we had to help them define what that meant.

"If I turn these buses back to retrieve you, I run the risk of everyone missing the ship. That would result in a loss of thousands of dollars as well as the cruise experience. If I turn these buses back, I am saying to everyone it really doesn't matter if you show up on time: We'll always be there to rescue you. If I turn these buses back, then I am rewarding your irresponsibility. I can't do that."

In truth, it felt really good.

"What am I supposed to do now?" came the puzzled and slightly frightened reply.

My response was simple: "Go Greyhound."

To the student's credit, he was waiting for us in Norfolk, Virginia, when the cruise ship returned. How he got there I never inquired. Together again, the ETC students continued their journey to Williamsburg to immerse themselves in one of the finest examples of "living history" anywhere in the world. Not a word was said about what had transpired. The point had been made. This story has become part of ETC lore. Students know that when we tell them to be somewhere on time, we mean it. It's not so much that we will leave you behind, as that you will miss the bus.

Chapter Six

Cancer: Act I

The turn of the century brought me something new: constant pain in my legs and a general feeling of malaise. I knew which direction the clock was ticking in, but was rather stunned to think that at the ripe old age of forty-seven my body was breaking down as quickly as it seemed to be. The demands of the ETC required many hours of commitment and work, especially as Randy and I were constantly reassessing our mission, curriculum, project structure, and individual roles—so this pain was something that simply had to be endured. I was too busy, and frankly a little too scared, to address it. Fortunately, the upcoming West Coast trip would take my mind off this physical annoyance.

The 2001 West Coast tour was going to be special because it would include the opening of Disney's newest theme park, Disney's California Adventure. This held even greater significance for Randy because planning for the park had been underway during his sabbatical at Disney a few years earlier. We'd see the culmination of what had been only a dream when Randy was there.

The day we arrived in Anaheim was simply gorgeous—sunny, crisp, and vibrant. The anticipation of the ETC students was palpable; they knew they were getting an early glimpse into Disney's newest wonderland. The park was in what is called "soft opening" mode, meaning it was open to visitors but had not yet officially opened to the general public. In theater we call this "previews."

Randy's good friend and colleague at Disney, Mk Haley, had arranged to show the ETC students an insider's view of the new park. We all awaited her arrival with bated breath, milling around the entrance, peering into the pristine new place, contemplating which rides and areas we'd explore and in what order.

It was then that I noticed I couldn't really walk. Suddenly, every step I took was marked by severe shin pain and leg cramps. I was moving like a geriatric, with gritted teeth and a perplexed and frightened look on my face.

Randy noticed. "What's the matter?" he asked.

"I don't know," I replied. "I can't seem to walk."

I concede that muttering that simple statement was a lot more dramatic than it looks in print. When I inquired once of a friend living in California about dealing with the ever-present earthquake threat, he replied, "You know Don, the Earth just isn't supposed to move. So, when it does, that is very scary." Well, the analogy applied to my legs: They *are* supposed to move! Mine moved, but only with excruciating pain.

At that moment the gates opened and the ETC students boisterously streamed into Disney's California Adventure. Randy and I watched them go forth; then we looked at each other.

"Are you going to be able to make it?" he asked.

"I don't know. I don't think I can walk the park at all. In fact, I think I just need to sit down, get off my feet. The shin pain is really bad." I was scared.

"Well, I'm not going to let you sit down by yourself. I'll sit with you," Randy replied.

"Randy, you've been waiting for this moment. Go ahead, join the students, see what your Disney colleagues created. I'll just sit here and have a cup of coffee," I urged him.

"No," was his immediate reply. "If you can't walk around and experience the park, then I won't go either. I'll sit with you. I can always come back and see it. We're in this thing together, remember."

I'm pretty sure I teared up, not only because of the sudden and frightening development in my body, but because of the extraordinary gesture on the part of my codirector. I knew this had to be a true sacrifice for Randy, a genuine disappointment. We pondered the strange illness that was sapping me of strength, but at the same time, I felt tremendous appreciation for the fact that Randy chose to attend to me in my illness rather than experience the joy of visiting the park. I was appreciative of his generosity of spirit then, and that appreciation grows with each recollection. His unselfishness touched me deeply. Happily for Randy, he had his laptop with him, so the time was not wasted.

Shortly after returning to Pittsburgh, I suffered a kidney stone attack. Further tests showed that I had an adenoma in one of my parathyroid glands. I remember well the doctor telling me this and my responding with, "Gee, thank goodness it isn't a tumor." To which he replied, "Well, an adenoma *is* a tumor, but of a secretion gland."

Oh.

Sensing my fear, the doctor spoke reassuringly, "I wouldn't be concerned, though, because these kinds of adenomas are almost never malignant." My exhalation said it all. "Still," he continued, "it needs to come out. So, we'll have to schedule an operation."

No one ever wants to hear those words, but at least there was an explanation to what had been ailing me. It turns out that when your parathyroid isn't working properly, fatigue, memory loss, and muscular aches and pains, especially in the shins, are the side effects. My wife, Jan, and I faced the pre-operative procedures with our share of anxiety and stress.

I don't recall Randy and I having too many conversations as my medical drama unfolded. He wasn't good with medical issues. That is why his amazing courage later, in the face of his own cancer, absolutely astonished me. Randy was someone who, if he had a sore throat, turned it into a federal case. He would phone in to say he feared a cold was coming on and he was going to stay home. I got the clear feeling that any deviation from good health worried him a great deal.

I kept Randy apprised of my medical developments in detail. I was very concerned that my illness would interfere with my responsibilities at the ETC. As I conveyed to him the date of the operation, along with a description of what the surgeon was going to do, I tried my best to replicate his stoic, highly logical and rational approach.

There are a lot of advantages to taking a rational and logical approach to one's medical situation. The idea was to subdue my psyche with reason, sparing myself any anxiety or emotional pain. Sometimes I managed to do this, and the concept of the mind/body duality was confirmed for me. But I was not able to sustain my logical attitude for long and was forced to confront not merely the mind/body connection but the spirit/body duality as well. Randy would be able to find consolation in the potential for science/medicine/mind to triumph over the weakness of the body's physical laws. I just simply wasn't that logical.

The details of my operation aren't that interesting, but suffice it to say that things did not go as planned. What was supposed to be a forty-five-minute operation during which the adenoma would be removed turned into a three-hour endurance test requiring an urgent call to an ear, nose, and throat specialist.

I sensed something was amiss when I woke up in the recovery room and was greeted by an unfamiliar face.

"You don't know me, but I operated on you," the distorted face said. "Can you speak?"

I think I muttered, "What the hell is going on?" to which he responded, "All right, good, that's what I needed to hear." I then fell back asleep, not sure if this was a dream or the recollection of a Marx Brothers movie.

The next thing I recall is waking up in my hospital room. My original surgeon came in to examine the stitched-up incision.

"I must be one of the few Italians ever to recover from a slit throat," I joked. This guy had no sense of humor; he continued examining his handiwork, muttering to himself about how beautifully he'd sewn me up.

"Did you do a biopsy?" I asked. The reply was not what I expected. He stopped what he was doing, jumped back a few feet, peered at me and said, "Why are you asking that?"

A smart-ass always, I retorted, "I don't know, just making conversation."

"The tissues have to be examined carefully by the pathologists before any determination can be made," he said, or something to that effect. I figured he, too, was a Mr. Spock wannabe, so I let it go at that.

Shortly after that, my personal physician came in and gently sat on the edge of my bed. Dr. Jerry Rabinowitz is truly one of the finest doctors imaginable. He has been our family doctor for more than twenty-five years and has always been a kind and caring yet straight-shooting physician. When Randy asked me if I knew of a good family doctor, I recommended Dr. Rabinowitz without a moment of hesitation. It was Dr. Rabinowitz who had the grim task, years later, of telling Randy that he had a malignant tumor in his pancreas.

"Don," he calmly began, "everyone has been waiting for me to talk to you."

I thought that was a very nice, though somewhat ambiguous, way to begin. It definitely caught my attention.

He continued, "The operation did not go as expected. The surgeon said he had never seen tissue like what he found in your neck. It was sticky, strange, oddly shaped, and had wrapped itself around the nerve controlling your vocal chords."

This was very significant. During my pre-operative interview with the surgeon, which is kind of like interviewing prospective insurance agents, I asked him what was the worst thing that could possibly happen during the operation, short, of course, of his suddenly losing his mind and going all Sweeney Todd on me.

"Well," he reflected, "your parathyroid glands are situated beneath your thyroid gland, and the nerve that controls your vocal chords is located right between them. Cutting that nerve would be a real problem for someone who speaks for a living."

Hmm, I thought, kind of like a professor or an actor, eh?

"Did he cut the nerve controlling my vocal chord?" I anxiously asked Dr. Rabinowitz.

"No," he reassured me, but the gravity of what he was hinting at hit me right between the eyes. When your doctor spends a lot more time looking at your bed sheets than into your eyes, you sense something is amiss.

"Are you telling me it might be cancer?" I whispered in a suddenly raspy voice.

"Yes."

I watched the room spin a few times, amazed at how quickly one's entire world could change. Cancer had been ever-present in my family life. My father had died of it back in 1983; my maternal grandmother died of it in 1976, and my maternal grandfather back in 1968. I was all too aware of the "Big C."

"Well, suppose it is cancer; what are my options?" I asked rather valiantly.

Dr. Rabinowitz thought for a moment, furrowing his brow, and then offered, "Well, we'd have to go in and cut it out."

"Well, the surgeon was just in there—didn't he cut it out?" I asked.

"You know, that's a good question," Dr. Rabinowitz replied in his classic understated fashion. "There's a good chance he did."

Those were very reassuring words to me, even as my brain tried to grasp the immensity of what had just transpired. Maybe I had had cancer, but not any more; talk about the good, the bad, and the ugly. I was left to contemplate the enormity of it all.

Recovery from the incision went quickly, much more so than the battery of follow-up tests. I went back to work, always a source of satisfaction for me, and conveyed the ongoing saga to Randy. He listened intently but dispassionately, as was his custom with anything medical. When the going gets tough, we all revert to our most comfortable way of being, and for Randy this always involved a scientific, highly rational approach. The world would later witness this when he calmly described the metastasis of his pancreatic cancer or the medical procedures undertaken to combat it.

Throughout the two months during which doctors attempted to figure out whether my cancer had spread and become life threatening, Randy was a reassuring and calming presence. I'd come in after each MRI or CAT scan emoting about the procedure, life, and all the ramifications of mortal illness, and Randy would greet me as a stalwart, rational, calming presence. His focus on the facts went a long way toward dispelling dark thoughts and gut-wrenching scenarios. His behavior was a testament to moderation of mind and character.

At one point, we shared a genuine, hard-core, tension-releasing belly laugh. I was recounting my MRI experience at a local hospital. Before you get an

MRI you have to go through a kind of preflight checklist, which comes in the form of a questionnaire. One question they ask is if you are claustrophobic.

Now, I have never had a problem with tight spaces. I have no trouble flying on small airplanes or taking elevators. I prefer not to be locked in closets, but I could survive it. So, I showed up for the MRI expecting to get through it like a trooper.

I lay down on the gurney slightly curious about the procedure but completely in control. Then they strapped me to the gurney like Frankenstein's monster. A helmet of some sort was placed on my head and ratcheted down like a palette on a cargo plane. I felt my blood pressure ever so steadily rising as they slid me into what could only be described as a torpedo tube. I was the torpedo. Then commenced some of the loudest pounding I had heard since a Jimi Hendrix concert I attended in 1969.

Lou Costello would have been proud of the hollering I did at that point. The nurse, clearly frustrated, extricated me from the MRI tube and said with only slightly disguised disgust, "I thought you said you weren't claustrophobic."

"I'm not claustrophobic," I countered vociferously through clenched teeth. "I don't have any problems with tight spaces like elevators. You didn't ask if I had any problem being strapped down like Houdini, inserted into a metal sewer pipe, and then enduring a sledge hammer pounding on the damn pipe as if I were a human glockenspiel. I would have told you straight up I might have a problem with that."

She sighed as if I were ruining *her* day. "So what we are going to do about this?" she asked in a tone I hadn't heard since my mother scolded me in third grade.

"I think I could get through it if there was some sort of distraction," I suggested.

"How about a cold compress over your eyes?"

"Sounds great to me," I cheerfully replied. "You know," I added, "It would be even better if there was some music."

"Oh, we have music," she replied.

"You do?"

"Yeah," she said, "but it's a pain to set up."

"I'll set it up happily," I volunteered, wondering how desperate the nursing profession had become to hire such compassionate souls as the one I had been blessed with here.

"No, I'll do it," she sighed.

After a bit of tinkering and stretching of wires, she asked me, "So, what do you want to listen to during the MRI?"

Considering my close encounter of the submarine kind, I figured I needed something loud. "How about ZZ Top?"

"Hmm, no ZZ Top," she said. "How about Yanni?"

Realizing we had now crossed from the sublime to the ridiculous, I said, "My dear, Yanni is what you listen to when you are in the anteroom of heaven. I'd like to think I have a few years before that. What do you have that's loud?"

She rummaged around and pulled out a treasure: "How about *Led Zeppelin's Greatest Hits*?"

"Bless you," was all I could reply. So, with a cold compress on my eyes and a headset blaring Led Zeppelin, I was inserted once again into the torpedo tube. This time, I made it all the way through. If only the banging of the machine had kept time with the music.

Randy and I had a good laugh over that experience. Despite his propensity for reason, when the going got tough, both of us valued the power of humor to release tension. Conceptually, this makes all the sense in the world because comedy—a major dramatic genre—is grounded in objectivity. Tragedy seeks to get us emotionally involved; but comedy works its magic by distancing us from the subject. Comedy is highly rational. It is one of the ways in which we learn of society's expectations and become able to withstand the vagaries, uncertainties, and unfairness of life. Thank goodness for comedy, especially when the news is bad!

I recall vividly the appointment with the surgeon in which all of the follow-up medical tests were to be evaluated and a definitive diagnosis rendered. Jan and I sat in the doctor's office anxiously awaiting his entrance. He didn't disappoint. The door opened. The white-robed figure entered. He walked across the room to the opposite wall, turned rather dramatically toward me, and stated matter-of-factly: "It was a malignancy."

I cannot state for certain that I know where the human soul is located, but the solar plexus would be a good guess, because at that moment I felt a veritable nuclear explosion go off in my body, beginning right below my sternum and radiating outward like the concentric circles a pebble creates when tossed into a still pond.

I was still stunned when my wife asked, "So what is the prognosis?" I fear I glared at her.

Of course, there was that pregnant pause precisely when I didn't need any additional drama. "Well, I think I got it all. So, you should be cured."

My emotional constitution is not strong enough to handle horror and joy almost simultaneously, despite my being a true-blue Gemini. I didn't know whether to cry or heave a sigh of relief. Part of me was still stuck on the "It was a malignancy" part of the discussion.

Eventually, his second statement sank in, although both Jan and I focused on the *should* part of it. "What do you mean I *should* be cured?" I asked.

"Well," he replied, "It is a slow-growing cancer, one that likes its original home. Cutting it out should do the trick."

Our mutual glee was curtailed by the follow-up statement.

"Still, you will need to go to an oncologist who can investigate further."

He gave me the name of an oncologist—who shall remain nameless for reasons that will become obvious—and we departed. I never did see the surgeon again.

Returning to the ETC, I recall conveying all of this to Randy. He listened to my stories like a scientist, showing little emotion, though clearly absorbing every word I said. He seemed as puzzled as I was and uncertain whether to commiserate about my bad luck or congratulate me on the good news. He seemed to be mentally calculating my odds of a good result. What seemed reassuring, though, was his glee in calculating those odds.

Randy reveled in the ability of the human brain to apply mathematical certainty to the real world. And for someone who really doesn't have this ability (someone like me), it was immensely reassuring to be in the company of someone who could discuss my condition without emotion. Come to think of it, that is precisely what we look for in a doctor, therapist, accountant, attorney, or anyone charged with viewing us from the perspective of an "other." There are times when we need to be objectified in order to see things—and ourselves—clearly. Randy was a master of objectivity.

Over the next month I was subjected to a series of tests ordered by the oncologist, without a doubt the single most personality-challenged fellow I have ever encountered. It took a physician friend of mine to explain that oncologists are considered the exterminators of medicine. Their job is straightforward: rid the body of cancer in any way possible.

The meeting with the oncologist to discuss the cumulative result of all this testing came off like a bad movie. Every test was happily normal, except for the very last blood test he reviewed. He then rather unceremoniously informed me that the cancer had returned and I needed another operation. I was stunned. It made no sense, considering all I had heard about parathyroid cancer. I was depressed and angry. It was as if we had been playing *Let's Make a Deal* and I had chosen door number three, behind which lurked, drum roll please: more cancer!

When I got home, I received a telephone call from Dr. Rabinowitz. He congratulated me on the good news about my test results. I didn't know how to respond. I think I muttered something along the lines of "huh?" but in a tone that aroused the doc's curiosity; clearly, he was expecting me to be nothing short of jubilant.

"How can you congratulate me when I have to have another neck operation?" I asked.

"What are you talking about?"

So, I told him how the oncologist had reviewed the test results and concluded the parathyroid cancer had returned.

Dr. Rabinowitz responded vehemently, "But it hasn't returned. In fact, that test result is good news! That means the other parathyroid glands are kicking in to regulate your body's calcium. They have to be working overtime until the parathyroid hormone and calcium levels return to normal."

All of this was really beginning to wear me down; I didn't know what was what, whether to feel happy or sad, relieved or angry, drink to celebrate or drown my sorrows.

Understanding at last what was going on, I informed Dr. Rabinowitz that I was done with that particular oncologist, that I would not talk, correspond, or have anything to do with him ever again.

It was very satisfying to convey all of this in stunning detail to Randy, because he remained stoic in the midst of my agitated, angry, and oftentimes irate retelling of these incredible tales. Looking back, comparing my cancer episode with Randy's, it is easy to see why Randy became a partner to his physicians as they monitored his condition, prognosis, treatment, side-effects, potential outcomes, and such. My wife, Jan, did that in my case, much more than I ever did. I basically didn't want to hear the truth. Call it denial if you will; I think it had much more to do with fear. Sickness is one circumstance, though, where I can say that the truth does make us free. Throughout his amazing battle with pancreatic cancer, I sensed Randy had the upper hand because he always knew what was going on in his body.

When I finished conveying the litany of convoluted facts and my seeming victory over a rare form of cancer, Randy pointed out that I was indeed lucky. That struck me as slightly odd because I had just gone through a horrific confrontation with the unknown, a diagnosis of a cancer so rare that I was the first case in thirty years at one of Pittsburgh's major hospitals. Yet, Randy was insisting that I was lucky. It took me awhile to grasp that he was right.

The fact of the matter is, I *was* lucky. There are many other cancers out there that I could have gotten, that would have meant very serious treatments and uncertain consequences. Of course, the irony was not lost on us when Randy was diagnosed in 2006.

Since that horrific episode, I have had time to consider my cancer with a degree of balance. I credit Randy's left-brain perspective on the matter with helping me toward enlightenment. Throughout his prolonged battle with pancreatic cancer, Randy expressed great admiration for the human spirit that was reflected in the care and concern he received, but he had always been the embodiment of this same spirit, especially in the way he helped me through my personal battle with cancer.

This life-changing experience taught me a great deal about the need for objectivity. As is usually the case with humor, emotional detachment allows one to see a situation more clearly. This, in turn, is the road to wisdom.

Chapter Seven

It's True! Two Halves Comprise the Whole

Once, while I was an undergraduate at the University of Tampa, I had a seemingly innocuous hallway encounter with a professor that had a lifelong impact on me. This young professor had recently completed all the requirements for his doctoral degree. His dissertation had been approved by his graduate school committee. All that was left was to receive the symbols of his accomplishment at the graduation ceremony, and he could adopt the moniker of "Ph.D." and be referred to as "Doctor." We, his students, were happy for him, as he was a fine teacher and a true scholar.

That auspicious day, he looked despondent—so much so that I asked him if something was wrong. He looked at me as if thankful someone had taken notice of his sadness. He described four years of arduous study, difficult classes, and intense research, all culminating in a dissertation of which he was intensely proud.

"So what's the problem?" I inquired.

"The problem is that having a Ph.D. will give people the impression that I actually know everything about my subject, that I am an expert, that I have 'arrived,' academically." He continued in a voice exuding angst. "But the truth of the matter is that I have never felt as ignorant as I do now. I feel as though I have barely scratched the surface of my subject." He let out a sigh and slowly shook his head.

I knew I was witnessing a moment of truth. Out here in the hallway, the classroom masquerade ceased. Our roles as professor and student melted away and we were just two individuals, separated by not too many years, sharing a harsh yet genuine reality.

There wasn't much I could say in reply. I muttered some pointless encouragement. He offered a half-smile, a broken grin, and disappeared into his office.

This incident shaped my own approach to higher education. I learned a very important lesson that day: I will always be more ignorant than I am smart.

The establishment of the ETC put me in a difficult situation with regard to teaching. As I've said, I am not a video game player, at least not in comparison to any young person who would be interested in the ETC. As a result, I was faced with the prospect of either faking my way through class or admitting ignorance. The latter proved to be one of the most liberating experiences of my life.

I boast nowadays of the liberation I feel walking in front of an ETC class and pronouncing to the students my now well-known tagline: "You all know more than I do about video games; I just happen to know more about everything else." I invite them to approach class as a partnership: "You teach me what you can about the thrill, enjoyment, satisfaction, frustrations, and aspirations of playing video games, and I will teach you the storytelling elements of plot, character, theme, diction, rhythm, and spectacle that help transform video games into a true art form."

This liberates the students as well. Early on, we found that it seemed to be easier to get artists and engineers to work together than to get engineers to work with each other. We wondered why that was the case. One thing that became obvious was everyone's ignorance of one another's skill sets. For the most part, students had no choice but to admit their lack of knowledge of the "other half." This tended to clear away egotistical attitudes triggered by the fear of comparison. Interpersonal relationships within the ETC were founded instead on intellectual curiosity, disciplined inquiry, project collaboration, and personal inclination. There was little opportunity for "my coding skills are better than your coding skills" comparisons, or bickering over artistic talent and capabilities. Most learning occurs through interactions among the students. These interactions are fundamental to the ETC program.

As leaders of this venture, Randy and I served as models of interactive collaboration. We quickly became the Carnegie Mellon version of Arnold Schwarzenegger and Danny DeVito in the movie *Twins*. Randy was the tall, dark, handsome, and debonair straight man; I was the short, stocky, loud comedian, always ready with a comic retort for any situation. In our organizational behaviors, we were also vastly different: I am a man-of-action, eager to get something done, or built; Randy was more the researcher and investigator, always seeking knowledge and potential applicability—although he, too, believed that nothing speaks louder than a working, demonstrable expression of technology, a tangible example of its possible benefit to humankind.

We realized quickly that we each had much to learn from the other. I daresay we wound up learning a great deal more about life than about our primary intellectual endeavors during our six years together, but we took to heart the adage that the best way to learn is to teach. In attempting to explain to each other the foundations of our own thought, how we approached problems, we gleaned keen insights into the workings of both the scientific and the artistic mind. While we promoted our codirectorship as the coming together of right-brain and left-brain thinking, the punch line was that it took two lobes to make a whole brain.

Randy always subscribed to the ETC mission of turning computer science into a performing art—and with good reason. Unlike most computer science professors, Randy loved the limelight. He could command an audience instinctively by tapping into their logical and rational inclinations. I, on the other hand, specialize in tapping into an audience's emotions. Together we truly covered the bases.

I'd also say that during the six years we shared an office, we proved to be each other's "brick wall," a term Randy used to describe life's obstacles. When one of us raised objections or opposition to an idea by the other, it inspired a more serious reflection and investigation into the true aims, goals, and objectives behind the suggestion. Everything had to be taken to the next level, accompanied by constant reflection on our personal and professional motivations.

The Randy I worked with in the early days of the Entertainment Technology Center was a much more conservative and cautious individual than the Randy known to the world through his Last Lecture. This aspect of his personality was transformed after receiving his pancreatic cancer diagnosis. It may be hard to believe for those who know him solely through the Last Lecture, but he always described himself as being "the most risk-adverse human being" he knew. While he was always an open-minded thinker when it came to social issues, and generally liberal when it came to politics and philosophy, he was genuinely risk-adverse when it came to practically everything else.

Randy proved to be an articulate, personable, daring visionary with a genuine sense of humor. He was so straight and wholesome that sometimes it was hard for me to recognize him as a fellow member of the human race; he was definitely not like anyone I had grown up with in Brooklyn or Miami. He didn't smoke, didn't drink alcoholic beverages (save for a ceremonial glass of wine every now and then), wouldn't be caught dead gambling, was a genuine workaholic, was astoundingly health-conscious (he worked out daily at the gym), played team sports, avoided eating spicy foods, never listened to rock-and-roll, had never even contemplated engaging in recreational pharmaceutical research, and proudly referred to himself as Pollyanna, while boasting to everyone who cared to listen that he considered himself a Tigger rather than an Eeyore. Randy was such an angel, I sometimes expected him to sprout wings.

I, in contrast, am a full-fledged Italian American from Brooklyn, a lifelong actor best suited to playing overweight Italian relatives or mafia hit men. As a kid, I watched Abbott & Costello movies convinced that Lou Costello was my real father! Trust me when I say no one in Bensonhurst ever walked around proudly proclaiming to be a Tigger. My salty personality has always been at odds with my academic accomplishments—but this dissonance has always bothered other academics more than it has me. Being the first one in my immediate family to attend college made me the object of much ribbing and teasing, whenever "book learning" seemed to conflict with the commonsense lessons my father had picked up on the streets of New York or the beaches and battlefields of the South Pacific.

I've already talked about Randy's habit of eating the same thing every day for lunch, a quirk he shares with my wife. Jan and I are time-capsule examples of the adage "opposites attract." It works at home, and it worked for me with Randy. Randy and I not only worked side by side, but we were "married" professionally, to each other and to this thing called the Entertainment

Technology Center. Randy boasted to our students that if he and I could share an office for six years, anyone could overcome the neurological divide and learn to work productively with the "other" half of the brain.

There were, of course, certain behaviors that were simply too extreme for either of us to accept in the other. Randy, for instance, found my theatrical habit of hugging everyone I meet as often and as long as possible to be, shall we say, off-putting and potentially politically incorrect. I didn't care.

Similarly, when he would go off on a Mr. Spock riff about human-computer interaction that mimicked a neurosurgeon explaining a pending procedure, my eyes glazed over. My personal impression was that both of our behaviors were in fact forms of affectation rather than any kind of hard-wired brain function.

Randy was once asked to describe how two such different individuals could get along so well. His answer was insightful, and was captured by Ann Curran in an article that appeared in *Carnegie Mellon Magazine*:

> If given a Myers-Briggs test, Pausch is convinced that Marinelli would come out as caring more about people's feelings, and he [Pausch] would "care much more about their rights . . . I'm much more concerned with process, and he's much more concerned with relationships. The great thing is that we have both of those. You find a way to work together and not kill each other." The pair has never, he says, "had a knockdown, drag-out fight."

When we reviewed applications for admission to the ETC together, for example, our similarities emerged. At least 80 percent of the time, we were simpatico in our decisions. And when we did disagree, it usually concerned test scores and grades. He was much more willing than I to take both at face value. For me, this was a gray area. My own GRE scores were abysmal, whereas my grades were always high. I was more willing to consider extenuating circumstances regarding less-than-stellar grades when countered by a highly intelligent, creative, heartfelt essay and/or intriguing portfolio. Randy was less forgiving in that regard. Both of us, though, would always listen to the rationale presented by the other. I'd say we changed each other's minds 50 percent of the time.

We each deferred in areas that simply were not specific to our expertise. I possess no comprehension of computer code; Randy demurred readily from looking at portfolios, although his design background and basic intelligence more than qualified him to comment upon readily accessible artistic elements such as space, shape, line, form, and texture. Still, he was not about to engage in a discussion regarding, for example, a candidate's use of negative space to enhance linear perspective.

Back in 2002, when the ETC was just hitting its stride and people in many disciplines discerned its visionary aspects, Randy and I were asked about the chemistry of our working together. In the same article quoted above, Ann Curran captured Randy's enthusiasm and his explanation of why the ETC was unique:

> Interestingly, Pausch, wearing the techno hat, presents the more impassioned explanation of what he and the ETC are doing. "I love being at Carnegie Mellon. I can't tell you how good it is to be here . . . Don and I approach things just radically differently, and for me personally the most exciting thing about [the ETC] is I get to work with Don. . . When I collaborate with people, the further apart they are from me, the more I learn . . . I don't want to say magical elixir, but we found what seems to be a sustainable formula for putting people from the arts and technology together."

I always enjoy reminding people that drama had techies long before computer science was ever invented. Even when plays were performed only during daylight hours, there was a wide variety of technologies used in live performances. Anyone studying Greek drama, for instance, learns about the various stage devices crafted by Greek theater technicians to enhance and augment the theatrical experience. Theater has always been a coming together of technology and dramatic artistry.

There is, however, a very important clarification that needs to be made here: In conventional theater, technicians, designers, and actors work in parallel, but they do not work together. If anything, the specific disciplines are exclusive. The costumers are off in the costume shop designing, crafting, and fitting costumes; the production crew is in the scene shop building the set; the lighting designers and electricians are in the theater hanging and focusing lights. Essentially, everyone is off doing his or her own thing.

The various disciplines finally come together during what we call "tech week." That is when the set, costume, lighting, sound, rigging, and all other technical aspects of the production are combined with the acting and the entire show comes together. It is usually the very first time everyone has a chance to see what the production is going to look like to audiences.

As a result of my experience in the theater, one thing I very much admire about the field of interactive digital media is that all disciplines within it are present all the time, usually in the same studio space, from the first day of work until the project launches. In my work at ETC, I have discovered at last a kind of collaboration that links one of the most ancient of artistic endeavors— storytelling—to the most amazing palette of presentation and performance techniques ever devised.

I always enjoyed Randy's penchant for weaving stories from personal experience, as it was my preferred manner of instruction as well. It was this shared method that led to the ETC's emphasis on experiential learning through myriad adventures, challenges, games, trips, visitors, and hands-on research and development utilizing as many of the technologies of the trade as possible and practical.

Randy often described his evolution as a teacher as a transformation from traditional lecturer to storyteller. Instead of factual compilations or bulleted PowerPoint presentations, Randy relied on presenting ideas via narrative. He sought to craft memorable characters within the stories he told, and strove always to include a discernible theme. In other words, he was following the fundamentals of good storytelling as enunciated by Aristotle in his seminal work *The Poetics*. No wonder Randy and I got along famously: He was a closet dramatist!

Randy was fond of referring to himself as a Pollyanna. Of course, I had heard the term before and understood its connotations—someone who always sees the bright side, even when common sense might dictate otherwise—but never had I heard anyone proudly pronounce *himself* a Pollyanna.

For those of you who are not literati, allow me to give a little background. *Pollyanna* is a best-selling 1913 novel by Eleanor H. Porter. It is important to note that you will find it at your local bookseller in the children's literature section. The book was so successful that it spawned something like a dozen sequels, some appearing as recently as the 1990s.

The title character's philosophy of life centers on what she calls "The Glad Game," an optimistic attitude she learned from her father, who taught her always to look at the good side of things and find something to be glad about in every situation. Pollyanna so loved to play this game that she became known as the Glad Girl. Randy could appropriately have been called the Glad Guy.

A Pollyanna is cheerfully optimistic and always maintains a generous attitude toward other people's motives. Where I grew up, however, Pollyanna had a negative spin, signifying a naive optimist who always expects people to act decently, despite strong evidence to the contrary. Learning how to reconcile these opposing perceptions was part of the challenge of Randy and me working together.

This was one more example of Randy short-circuiting a presumption I had made about him. He had done this a number of times before, most notably when he admitted that he enjoyed knitting.

"Knitting?" I replied in a hushed voice.

"Oh yes," he said, as if it were the most normal thing in the world for an Übermensch to take up knitting. He raved about the manual exercise and precise hand-eye coordination involved, and about the lovely objects he could make as gifts. I listened intently. After all, I had spent most of my life in the theater and knew a few guys who enjoyed knitting. None of them, however, was also a renowned computer science geek, letter-jacket school athlete, and recognized lady-killer. As was becoming all too common, the more I found out about Randy, the more intrigued I became.

Randy was the absolute embodiment of Pollyanna attributes—usually to my personal befuddlement and wonder. For example, I don't ever recall Randy being genuinely angry. He could most certainly become frustrated and perplexed by people's actions—but truly angry, no. He was always willing to give someone the benefit of the doubt, even while I was busy measuring that person for a noose. He embodied the word patience.

Yet, Randy's mantra to me—his antidote to my constant suspicions of people's motives—was always, "Never attribute to malice what might just as easily be explained by ignorance." Those words always shook me up but good.

I have learned to take that advice to heart, though—thanks to Randy. It has become a new commandment for me, one that pops into my head whenever I feel myself descending into self-assured biases and prejudices. That attitude of generosity toward others is one of the many gifts Randy gave me as we lived side by side those six years.

During Randy's Last Lecture, he talked about his preference for Tigger over Pollyanna. In fact, he gave Tigger more publicity than the manic tiger has received since the re-release of *Winnie the Pooh*. For Randy's memorial service at Carnegie Mellon, the university purchased hundreds of stuffed Tigger dolls, which were placed on every chair in Rangos Hall. It was a Tigger paradise, and the university encouraged those in attendance to take a Tigger with them as they left the service.

Tigger's opposite number is Eeyore, the donkey character from *Pooh*. Eeyore feels the weight of the world on his shoulders; he is caught up in life's unfairness and irrationality; he is oppressed by existential angst and questions the very meaning of life. Randy was most definitely not an Eeyore.

My own A. A. Milne character is not so clear. Must we all choose between life as a Tigger or as an Eeyore? Randy and I diverged on this fundamental question. I admit to being both, sometimes simultaneously! The vagaries of life, the demands of home and office, the pressures of the outside world, and the impact of forces beyond our control create for me a maelstrom of mixed emotions. I believe that the question of whether it is better, wiser, healthier, or more fully human to commit to an unwaveringly positive outlook remains open for most of us.

One of Randy's group-dynamic mantras, an outlook and attitude he preached both in and out of class, was to avoid conflict at all costs. His reasoning was logical: Since the goal of the ETC was to foster group dynamics and teamwork, identifying transgressions and placing blame had no place. It was necessary to defuse tension, regardless of who was at fault in any situation. Randy called on all of us to be peacemakers since it always takes two to have an argument. Whenever tensions resulted in conflict, his advice was for the instigator to "apologize for upsetting your peers."

Randy and I differed considerably on this point. I recognized his outlook as intrinsically Christian, although Randy would categorize it as intrinsically humanistic. I admit to my fully human inability to live up to his standards. In my defense, I'd say that I have always accepted the dramatic quality of existence. In theater we insist that the essence of drama is conflict. Most people live—or aspire to live—a dramatic life, absorbed as we all are in our own stories and those of others.

Stories are, for the most part, compressed expressions of our conflicts. They showcase our lives with all the boring parts removed. Unfortunately, peace is usually associated with boring. As a result, history becomes a chronological compilation of human conflict.

I can attest that starting a new academic program within the strictures, requirements, and bureaucracy of a large university will undoubtedly result in conflict, arising from competing administrative and personal agendas, changing rules, altered missions, financial realities, and myriad other questionable motivations.

I consider bureaucracy to be the enemy of innovation. Unfortunately, colleges and universities can be as administratively top-heavy as government. When the Entertainment Technology Center was first created, the proposal by then-Provost Paul Christiano was that it should report to both the dean of the School of Computer Science (SCS) and the dean of the College of Fine Arts (CFA).

The challenge for us was figuring out how to be a part of the system we were setting out to change. We understood that we somehow had to fit into the existing structure of the university, but our goal was to be as independent as possible, since we were charged with breaking the mold of traditional education.

A proviso had been written into the ETC's charter whereby we would be solely responsible for our curricular and financial decisions. If the time came when the ETC was no longer able to attract students willing to pay tuition, find jobs for our graduates, or pay our way within the university, then we would close up shop. Randy and I accepted the challenge of creating this new center without any outright support from the university's central administration. We agreed to run the ETC like a business and to take responsibility for all aspects of its operation, a radical notion in not-for-profit higher education.

In 1999, we expressed our desire to report directly to the provost instead of the deans of SCS and CFA. This would allow us to fulfill our mandate of breaking the mold, to create a center that functioned differently from any traditional academic department. If we were going to lead the charge toward a new teaching methodology, we first had to get out from under the traditional hierarchical structure. Fortunately, in Provost Mark Kamlet we found a visionary who sensed the uniqueness of the ETC and was willing to entrust Randy and me with the authority and responsibility to guide the center as we saw fit

As his "roommate" for six years, I got to see Randy's time management skills in action. It might be a slight exaggeration to say that Randy lived his entire life by a schedule, but he came close. He tended to structure every facet of his day and then carried out each task in his own inimitable style. Suffice it to say, this attribute of Randy's was about as distant from my own stance toward time management as one could possibly get.

Randy committed himself to time management long before cancer rendered every second of his life precious. He always placed immense value on getting the most out of every waking moment. He was never bored; in fact, boredom made absolutely no sense to him (nor does it to me).

Our different approaches to time management made for some very funny situations. One time we were in the midst of an animated conversation when suddenly Randy stopped talking. He had just remembered something important. His left arm came up to his mouth and he began to speak directly into his wristwatch in a clipped, staccato manner. He returned to our discussion mid-sentence without missing a beat.

It was my turn to stop the dialogue. "What just happened?" I asked.

"Oh," Randy replied, "You know, my memory isn't very good, so I bought this combination wristwatch/recorder. That way I can record thoughts and recollections as they come to me. I can also remind myself to do things." Then, I think he actually winked. He was gleefully proud of his new toy. "Pretty nifty, eh?"

"I've only seen those in old Dick Tracy cartoons," I replied. Randy smiled proudly. "Just out of curiosity, are you going to do that in public?" I inquired. "You know, start talking into your wristwatch?"

"I might," he said. "Why?"

"Because," I went on, "there are plenty of people out there who are going to consider that very nerdy."

"You really think it's nerdy?" he asked. I just rolled my eyes.

For the next few months he continued to record thoughts, appointments, messages, and phone numbers, in public and in private, despite every look, sigh, or raised eyebrow coming at him from my desk. The wristwatch disappeared only after Randy found an even better gadget to take its place.

Randy found remarkable my natural ability to remember appointments, meetings, and to-dos. I would write things down on scraps of paper and attach them with tape to my desk, file cabinets, and shelves—which drove him mad. He was not one for organized chaos, whereas I thrive on it.

"What kind of a calendar system is *that*?" he would exclaim.

"It works for me," I'd boldly defend. "Besides, I get great satisfaction from ripping down a scrap of paper after an appointment or task is completed, tearing it into little pieces, and throwing it in the trash." Randy would just shake his head in bewilderment. You could say we were even.

Thinking back on our six years together, I see many more similarities between us than I do differences. And what differences there were, were really more semantic than substantive. Randy's extreme focus on time management complemented my juggling of strategic vision and tactical implementation. For instance, I am a very big fan of teleological thinking. This can be defined as consequential thinking: "What might happen if I take this particular action?" The goal of such thinking is to predict the consequences out to as many decimal places as possible. This kind of thinking clearly comes into play in chess games, but also is applied in politics and even on a date. It is engaged in with an eye always on the temporal dynamic. Being in the right place at the right time often requires the strategic manipulation of both of these elements.

Teleology is the basis of algorithmic thinking. Algorithms are extrapolated "if/then" equations: if X happens in accordance with the variables A, B, and C, then a specific action or state will result. Well, get ready for a revelation, because this is precisely what we artists do as well. The difference is that computer scientists build algorithms based on mathematics whereas the artist builds if/then propositions based on human psychology, literature, and language. The former is definitely more precise and thus more left-brain; the latter is more imprecise and thus more right-brain. But really, the same processes are taking place, just in different contexts, toward different ends. They are both attempts to create cause-and-effect relationships. They manipulate probability. They inject a degree of certainty into an uncertain world. Randy and I came to understand and appreciate this similarity in our thinking throughout our time together.

Chapter Eight
Cancer: Act II

Toward the end of 2005, I noticed that Randy seemed distracted and short-tempered (at least for him). I attributed it to the cumulative effects of fatherhood, which Randy had come to relatively late in life. And then, of course, there were the demands of sharing an office with a tornado.

Randy's family life and mine were heading in diametrically different directions. My only child, Olivia, was then eighteen years old, firmly established in high school and looking forward to college. She was determined *not* to go to Carnegie Mellon, as she wanted to establish her individuality and make her own discoveries. She was absorbed in her life of friends, plenty of homework, and a loving, caring mother in Jan, who attended to her needs in the finest maternal fashion. I was your all-too-common distant paternal figure, constantly traveling and obviously putting my career and work life above that of home and family—all mistakes.

While the ETC had become the central focus of my energy, Randy was contending with two young children and all that parenthood entails. I perceived the impact of this change in a strain lying just beneath the surface of Randy's usually upbeat demeanor. He became agitated more easily at work, though never belligerent. Instead, he appeared distracted and grew visibly frustrated whenever a decision required more than an immediate yes or no. For Randy, the ETC seemed to be fading into the background as family matters competed with his academic responsibilities.

While I was allocating long hours and much mental energy to strategic decisions involving the ETC, Randy was desperately trying to adhere to his time-management principles in fulfilling all the demands on his time. The result was increased tension between the two of us, which didn't sit well with me at all. We started having disagreements about the strategic direction of the program; Randy would respond to my suggestions with either a perfunctory agreement or a hasty veto, unwilling to engage in the creative dialogue that had characterized our working relationship up to this point.

During this period, I became increasingly amazed at the attraction of the world's youth to digital media. Students of all ages, cultures, backgrounds, races, and career interests were now seriously into video games, Japanese anime, manga, comics, and multiplayer online communities of all shapes, sizes, and genres. It appeared that interactive digital media had become the universal language of the young. Not surprisingly, the majority of ETC applications started coming from outside of the United States.

Around this time, we were approached by the Government of the State of South Australia to consider establishing a branch campus of the ETC Down Under in its capital of Adelaide. On the heels of this came a similar inquiry from the Singapore Economic Development Board. As a result, I embarked on a series of international trips to investigate the possibilities of satellite programs, as well as other potential global relationships. I took to these prospects with gusto, so much so that it unnerved Randy. Expanding the global signature of the ETC conflicted directly with his own desire to spend more time at home with his wife, Jai, and the kids. Storm clouds were developing between us.

When Randy referred to me as the Tornado in his Last Lecture, it was a pretty accurate description of my standard way of moving through life. I had grown up in a household where we argued constantly, and that instilled in me the habit of calling things as I see them and addressing problems head-on. Some view this kind of straight-shooting as being negative, uncaring (when the opposite is in fact the case), confrontational, accusatory, or, depending upon their cultural upbringing, loud.

When I was an adolescent, friends who came to my house were amazed at the volume at which my family and I communicated, and were stunned by the freewheeling language that peppered our conversation. I recall one unsuspecting date asking me to drop her off at church after spending an afternoon with us—she apparently felt the need to go to confession.

This predilection of mine to question and challenge almost everything led to one of the more serious incidents between Randy and me. During a faculty meeting, our then–program coordinator mentioned that he had been meeting with ETC faculty members to get their insights and comments about issues he deemed important. This upset me because one thing Randy and I always promised was an open-door policy to faculty, staff, and students alike. We believed the freedom to come forth and discuss any matter of concern was a matter of academic integrity, and key to the success of a program built upon right-brain/left-brain communication. So when I discovered that this staff member was taking it upon himself to solicit input from faculty that would support his agenda, I had a real problem. At the meeting, I went around the table asking faculty members one by one why they had not come to Randy or me with their concerns. I reiterated that anyone with issues concerning the leadership of the ETC should bring these matters to our attention. They could all see how agitated I was, although I didn't consider my behavior to be outrageous in the least. I was simply expressing my feelings directly and starkly.

When we returned to our office, however, Randy was ashen and clearly shaken. "You can't talk to people that way," he said, practically trembling.

I believe my reply was, "Huh?" I knew I had been loud and confrontational, but didn't really see the harm in that approach, given the circumstances.

"You chastised people in there," he said. "And you did it publicly."

In defense, I countered, "Excuse me. I pointed out behaviors that if left unchecked would segue right into the usual backbiting, hearsay, and gossip-mongering that fly in the face of open communication." It was very clear that Randy and I had different points of view. It was also clear that Randy was much more disturbed by the incident than I was, and this did bother me greatly.

This matter came to be known between us as the "Don the Werewolf" episode. At Randy's insistence, I issued an apology to the faculty and staff members who had been present.

Randy's insistence on avoiding confrontation at all costs was a veritable mantra for him. I, on the other hand, believe there are times when confrontation is definitely warranted. Randy perceived my approach as angry, while I perceived his as ambivalent. Indeed, during the episode detailed above, he had said nothing. To his mind, the Tornado had struck again, and had done so without warning.

All of this reminded me of the time Randy suggested I change my email address. Long before the founding of the ETC, I had been given the email address "thedon@cmu.edu" by a drama student who viewed this designation as truth in advertising. You see, I had developed a reputation over the years as the go-to guy in the School of Drama; the person who got things done. Plus, being an Italian guy from Brooklyn in an era of *Godfather* movies made this a humorous nickname with just the right amount of double entendre.

Randy's suggestion that I change this to a generic address took me by surprise. "Why should I do that?" I asked.

"So you don't scare people," he replied. I was incredulous. "Randy," I countered, "anyone who is afraid to send me an email because my address is 'the don' isn't someone I want to speak to anyway. I consider that cowardice of the highest order. The answer is no."

Curt exchanges like this one, though, were few and far between. Our shared purpose in making the ETC bridge the gap between art and technology, academia and industry, and help students realize their entrepreneurial dreams and aspirations kept us aligned in practically every way. Family matters outside of the ETC were about to change all of that.

One day that autumn, Randy came into the office looking especially depressed. He hurried to his desk. He sat down and just stared out the window. Maybe he was gazing at the waters of the Monongahela River that pass beneath our window, or at the cloud formations rolling across Pittsburgh's Mount Washington. While I would usually just let someone in this frame of mind rest in his solitude, this was so unusual for Randy that I had to ask him what was wrong.

"My dad has leukemia," was all he said.

He didn't have to say more. I knew how devastating this had to be for Randy. Randy's relationship with his father looked to me like the epitome of father-son love, genuine bonding, and mutual respect. In truth, I was flat-out jealous of it. Whenever Randy would detail a visit home to his folks' house in Maryland, or a vacation that included his extended family, I would experience a depressing sense of loss, sadness, and childlike envy. These family gatherings almost always seemed to result in wonderful memories and hilarious tales of family fun. It was difficult for me to frame a smile as I listened to what I had so very seldom experienced.

While I have always thanked God that my final words to my father were "I love you," it was in truth a deathbed reconciliation, overturning twenty years of estrangement. It was an act of forgiveness in its purest form that in no way mitigated the decades lost to fierce fights and physical and mental separation.

I could not imagine how Randy would deal with the sudden, devastating reality of his father's illness on top of the ever-changing demands of married life, parenthood, and the rapidly evolving ETC.

In a preview of his own battle with cancer, Randy rapidly became an expert on leukemia. He read everything on the Web about the disease, researched the variety of treatments available, and checked in daily to see how his dad was responding. He seemed to calculate on an almost daily basis exactly how much time he had left with his dad, based on the most recent test results and doctor's prognosis. I was in awe of the sense of responsibility Randy felt toward his parents.

There are only so many hours in the day, though, and only so much energy in the body. Randy's attention span for ETC business was becoming shorter and shorter. My frustration over his decreased concentration was increasing the tension in our relationship, albeit just under the surface.

One day I initiated a discussion about some idea I had for a new ETC initiative. Randy cut me off brusquely, so I replied with a sarcastic comment of my own. All of a sudden, Randy turned away and said, "I can't do this anymore."

I didn't quite know what he meant. Perhaps he was simply unwilling to engage me in debate; perhaps he was taking a stand in disagreement with my idea. While I tried to figure out where to go from there, he turned to me and said, practically through tears, "My dad is dying. I can't do this anymore."

I understood then that, in the face of his personal situation, the responsibilities of the ETC had become secondary. He was also offering me some insight into the nature of a meaningful father-son relationship. It began with mutual lifelong respect, strengthened by the fact that Randy always included his father in his academic and professional activities. There was no gulf between the two of them based upon differing interests. He was quick to seek his father's advice on whatever matter was at hand. They related as two adults. In addition, I sensed no vying between his parents for Randy's affection. The love seemed truly unconditional. Randy was proud that his father was always interested in new ideas. He could share the work being done in the ETC with his parents and receive genuine reaction and feedback.

I secretly marveled at his ability to come to value his work as secondary. I had not been as smart or level-headed fifteen years earlier, when Jan and I lived through a very troubled pregnancy that resulted in the stillbirth of our second child, a son we would name Rex. For years afterward, I would boast of the fact that throughout that horrific time—the baby survived for almost forty days in utero after the doctors told us he had only three or four days to live—that I had missed only one day of classes in the drama department. I thought of this as a badge of honor.

While my devotion to work was clearly a defense against the horrific trauma invading our life, in hindsight I lament the time I could have spent with my wife, attending to young Olivia's needs, or helping out at home while Jan dealt with this shocking nightmare. Randy was not going to make that mistake. As meaningless as it sounds now, I was truly proud of him. For Randy, family would absolutely come first.

Randy decided that he would step down as codirector of the ETC at the end of December 2005 to devote himself more fully to his family and also to his Alice project—Randy had always loved Alice. This meant that he could resume his routine of walking to work on the main campus and attend to his remaining doctoral students, while still being close enough to home to pop in whenever Jai needed a break from their two young children. Professionally, he would be able to focus exclusively on the Alice project, which, as demanding as it may have been, did not come with external sponsors and the needs of a student body of more than a hundred and growing. He also would no longer have to deal with the Tornado on a daily basis.

While it is true that the only constant in life is change, it is also true that growth is optional. I was determined to figure out whether I had grown during the eight years of sharing offices first with Scott Stevens and then with Randy Pausch. Had I really connected with my left brain? In other words, had I become whole?

Chapter Nine
The Post-Randy ETC

Randy's decision to step down as codirector meant that we'd have to figure out a new structure for the ETC. Should I seek out another computer science professor to replace him or attempt to steer the ship solo, with the help of existing and additional faculty?

Coming from a lifetime in drama, I had always admired and wished to emulate theatrical impresarios like Sergei Diaghilev and David Belasco. An impresario is a person who organizes or manages public entertainments, such as operas, ballets, or concerts, but he is also a promoter or showman. The word derives from *impresa*, the past participle of the Italian verb *imprendere* (to undertake). My tenure at Carnegie Mellon had certainly been filled with many undertakings, from theater festivals to the Moscow Art Theater Initiative to the Master of Arts Management Program. But the ETC was definitely the most innovative up to that point.

Against this background, after much thought and reflection, I suggested to Randy that I lead the ETC solo. Retiring the title of codirector like a revered baseball player's jersey number, I would take on the title of executive producer. Now, there aren't any executive producers in academic environments, at least as far as I am aware, but the title resonated with me. ETC projects resemble singular green-lighted endeavors, similar in nature to the multiple projects in production at a movie studio at any given time. My goal in taking this title was to underscore that the ETC functions much more like a Hollywood studio (or a grand, academic version of Willy Wonka's chocolate factory) than any kind of traditional academic entity. And, of course, therein lies the excitement for young people aspiring to careers in the entertainment industry.

While the prospect of becoming an impresario played a role in my eagerness to take the helm of the ETC, there was a more important reason why I felt prepared for the job. I had spent six years sharing an office with the most communicative, open, and insightful computer scientist I had ever known. Our relationship had been built on each of us teaching the other as much as possible about our individual disciplines. For six years I had peppered Randy with questions that surely drove him insane at times.

It is a testament to Randy's patience that he always responded to my incessant inquiries with professorial integrity. Over the years, through the process of osmosis and direct inquiry, I came to understand the structure of the mental process of the computer scientist, if not the specific content. In other words, the education we were aspiring to provide students in the ETC had taken hold in me as well. This was an exciting realization, akin to finally comprehending a foreign language after years of studying.

Right-brain/left-brain leadership had defined the ETC from its inception and had come to symbolize the center's uniqueness. The question now became whether it still required that kind of directorship. I believed the answer was no. I felt I had been an attentive student over the years, starting when Scott Stevens and I first shared an office and continuing through the years when Randy and I worked (and practically lived) side by side.

My personal evolution into what I can only call a whole-brain thinker mirrored that of the very generation we were welcoming into the ETC. It became increasingly evident by the second year of the program's existence that young people were already bridging the right-brain/left-brain divide by pursuing innovative academic paths during their undergraduate years. We were encountering double majors in many diverse disciplines. We'd read an application and discover that the applicant had double-majored in computer science and art, or created a major that combined electrical/computer engineering and design or math and creative writing. It seemed as if a great many young people were combining interests in science and art, and those permutations left Randy and me excited, enthused, and ultimately hopeful. The new generation was instinctively using both sides of their brains. I didn't know if parents had become more lenient, insightful, or liberal, or if young people were simply insisting on an education that better reflected their experience of life in a technology-mediated world. All I knew was that it resonated as right and proper for the time.

The infusion of young people who embraced multidisciplinary thinking made ETC projects more relevant, and largely self-sustaining. Our goals and objectives rose to a new level. Suddenly the aspiration to undertake projects that could impact the world no longer sounded grandiose. In fact, we wanted nothing more than to facilitate and guide the honest aspirations of our students.

The ETC remains an environment where learning is horizontally pervasive (among the students) and vertically transferred (between the faculty, staff, and students). No semester is ever the same because the projects differ. We take the expression "change is inevitable" and make it a mantra.

It has become very clear that the ETC has tapped into the most powerful source of education ever devised: the students themselves. The right-brain/left-brain mix that Randy and I had embodied as codirectors would continue to live in the composition of the students and in the curriculum.

Back in 2002, when ETC student Amy Kalson was asked by *Carnegie Mellon Magazine* editor Ann Curran how the ETC had prepared her for a career in the video game industry, she replied, "Brenda Harger's Improv class taught me invaluable teamwork and brainstorming skills. The ETC project cycles taught me how to thrive under very tight deadlines. I've learned as much from my peers as I have from my professors." Randy and I both thought Amy's comments constituted high praise for our approach.

We felt great pride when students "got" the educational mission of the ETC in practical ways. In the same article, ETC alumnus Shawn Patton was asked how the ETC had prepared him to work in interactive digital media. His reply became a perfect marketing sound-byte for the program: "All the programming

I learned at Rutgers helps me with the technical aspects, but the ideas of interactivity in game play I learned at the ETC, as well as the understanding of how the art aspects of projects mesh with the technical ones."

ETC student Dan Schoedel echoed Patton's sentiments: "The ETC taught me how to work with the computer science students. In addition, the ETC gave me great exposure to the tools used in this industry."

While Randy supported the idea that I would remain in charge as executive producer of the ETC, he felt a responsibility to delineate in detail, but with compassion, those personality and behavioral traits of mine that he and others had found problematic.

It wasn't easy listening to this litany or accepting his specific suggestions for personal improvement. Randy was a very self-assured individual, but we didn't always agree on what behavior was warranted. (I didn't take Tigger as my role model in all situations!) I conceded, however, that I owed it to him—and to everyone who would be affected by this change in leadership—to listen.

Imagine my surprise then when Randy proudly proclaimed, "I don't have any moods; I am always in control of my feelings," and sat there beaming like the cat that caught the canary.

"What do you mean you don't have any moods?" I asked incredulously.

"I can control my behavior so that I always project a happy mood," he declared.

"And that's healthy?" I exclaimed, my agitated demeanor living up to every definition of "moodiness." Randy sat there stoic, smiling, and completely in control. Both of us then burst out laughing. We just had to laugh on these occasions, finding our vigorous justifications inherently funny—and predictable. Randy was going to be Tigger no matter what. I continued to resemble the great Foghorn Leghorn, or some other loud, demonstrative cartoon character, forever hoping that verbosity and volume would prove an adequate pressure valve. Our different attitudes seemed to reflect the ontological complexity of being human—and that felt remarkably refreshing and honest.

I refuse to perceive either Randy's extremes of behavior or my own as the "proper" way to move through life. As a result of our discussions, I have, however, tried to tone down behaviors that in drama (and Brooklyn) were considered acceptable but that left-brain thinkers (and non–New Yorkers) might perceive as irrational or threatening.

As the fall semester of 2005 ground to a close, Randy met personally with President Jared Cohon and Provost Mark Kamlet to tell them of his decision to step down as codirector of the ETC. Afterward, he and I met with Mark to explain the proposed new structure. Happily, the provost gave his blessing, citing our tremendous accomplishments over six short years. He approved my new title, all the while acknowledging that he knew of no other university that had an executive producer of any academic division. All I could think was, *Another first for Carnegie Mellon!*

I'm sure you've heard the old adage, "Be careful what you wish for—you just might get it." With Randy's departure at the end of 2005, I entered 2006 flying solo; the ETC would now be mine to guide and nurture. Fortunately, Randy and I had assembled a terrific faculty and staff, and while there were certain individuals who felt more at ease with Randy than with me, and some turnover occurred as a result, the core group made the transition more smoothly than I ever could have imagined. We also grew the faculty and staff ranks significantly, reflecting the continuing expansion of the program due to our growing worldwide recognition and demand. Drew Davidson was brought on board as program director for ETC-Pittsburgh, while I focused on global expansion and ever more project sponsors.

It was comforting knowing that even though Randy would no longer be a part of the daily operation or strategic decision-making of the ETC, he would always be there for me—and I wouldn't need the bat signal to get hold of him. He'd either be working in his computer science office, discussing Alice enhancements with Dennis Cosgrove in the Stage 3 lab, or at home with his family. All I had to do was pick up the phone or send him an email. That was very reassuring.

One initiative I was determined to make a front-burner item in 2006 was the establishment of an ETC branch campus in the San Francisco Bay Area. Silicon Valley is the undisputed world center of video game development and the place most ETC students ultimately aspire to reside. I also viewed a Silicon Valley presence as the ETC's Pacific Rim outpost, since so much of the interactive digital media industry can trace its origins and ongoing development to Asia.

The goal of establishing a Silicon Valley presence became somewhat problematic, though, because Randy had spent a semester in residence at Electronic Arts (EA) in Redwood City, California, without moving us in that direction. Electronic Arts at the time was the largest video game company in the world. Randy was a tangible ETC presence at EA, underscoring the ETC's interest in learning as much as we could about the needs of video game companies from an undisputed leader in the industry. We were committed to turning out graduates ready to join the video game industry by all means possible, including osmosis! Yet, at the conclusion of Randy's EA residency, there was no movement or mention of an ETC-Silicon Valley. I was flustered by what I had felt was a lost opportunity.

During Randy's one-semester "externship" at EA, I had been the sole resident codirector in Pittsburgh while Randy was the invaluable "outside eye" on the workings of Electronic Arts. He ended up writing an important document for them titled *An Academic's Field Guide to EA*. Not having Randy around made it a bit difficult for us to make decisions jointly, and when he returned I asked, "So, what happened to the idea of an ETC-Silicon Valley?" He looked at me, puzzled. "I thought you were there to help establish an ETC in Silicon Valley," I said.

Randy surprised me by his answer: "I don't want to live in Silicon Valley."

"Who said you had to live in Silicon Valley?" I replied. "I never thought this was about you relocating." This was turning out to be one of the biggest disconnects of our time together. "I thought the idea was that a presence in Silicon Valley would give our students a leg up on the competition; that it would put us in closer contact with the companies we want hiring our grads. Once we agree on that, we can proceed with the question of who should be the on-site director."

It all seemed logical to me, but Randy could not see past his concern that running a Silicon Valley campus would take him and Jai far away from their families on the East Coast. As a result, the question of establishing an ETC-Silicon Valley was put on hold for the time being.

Once Randy made family his primary focus, the strategic vision of the ETC became my concern alone. Interactive digital media had established itself as the common language of young people all over the world, and I came to see myself as the entertainment technology evangelist. My mission became that of rallying politicians, academicians, and students the world over to the cause of merging entertainment and education. It was not that the idea that learning should be both fun and effective was unique to us. In fact (as I quoted earlier but can't resist repeating), no less an authority than Marshall McLuhan had astutely declared, "Anyone who thinks there is a difference between entertainment and education doesn't know much about either."

While Randy was settling down in Pittsburgh I was revving up the concept of "ETC-Global." As applications began arriving from all corners of the world, the attraction of video games, themed entertainment, and related endeavors among the world's youth was overwhelmingly clear. The world was knocking on our door and I was going to open it. This coincided with Carnegie Mellon's decision to become a global university with substantive initiatives in Europe, Asia, Australia, and the Middle East.

Yet, for all the travel, hoopla, interviews, articles, television stories, and other attention that the ETC garnered around the world, there remained no place like home. Pittsburgh is a welcoming city, a city that calls you back after being away. Tony Bennett may not have left his heart in *Pittsburgh*—but he could have. Even though I love to travel, I always yearn to return to the confluence of the three rivers.

Home for me was also the ETC. My entire life has been a merger of work with play. I have always taken to heart the belief there should be as little differentiation as possible between the two. Clearly, loving what you do at work is key to having a meaningful life—that's a no-brainer. Loving my work is certainly paramount to me, and I have been fortunate enough to have loved practically every job I have had as an adult. Of course, all of them have been in university education.

Coming home to Pittsburgh and the ETC meant the luxury of my office with the amazing view of downtown Pittsburgh, Mt. Washington, and the Monongahela River. I could watch the clouds roll in from the west or creep over the horizon from the south. The only difference was that for the first time in eight years (counting the two I spent with Scott Stevens) I would not be sharing an office with a computer scientist. I just hoped I had learned enough during my apprenticeship to be worthy of my new position, title, and responsibility.

What I came to see as most rewarding was sharing this adventure with a dedicated team of faculty and staff. Their sole focus was to create the most nurturing and enriching academic environment possible. It is true that when opposites attract they can create an even greater whole. To sustain the whole, there comes a time when it is necessary to find like-minded individuals who embody the same philosophy and purpose. To achieve a unified vision, all team members must have hearts dedicated to a single purpose, a purpose that becomes almost spiritual in nature.

Chapter Ten
Cancer: Act III

On September 11, 2006, I finished up a jam-packed Monday in the ETC and headed down to PNC Park to catch the Bucco game. Another academic year had begun. There was the usual rush and demand of getting to know the new students, making sure ETC projects had commenced with enthusiasm and focus, preparing for upcoming Adventure Modules, and the myriad other issues, decisions, opportunities, and surprises that marked the beginning of a new semester. It had been a long day and my mood was heavy, due in part to the significance of the date—the anniversary of my generation's Pearl Harbor.

As I walked across the Clemente Bridge, I vividly recalled that fateful day five years earlier. I had been riding in the Wean Hall elevator on my way to the ETC "Penthouse" in Doherty Hall. An acquaintance got in at one of the intermediate floors and asked excitely if I had heard about the airplane that crashed into the World Trade Center.

Her words did not compute at first, because just two days before that fateful morning, I had been in Manhattan with the entire ETC class on one of our grander field trips. We had embarked on a one-night cruise-to-nowhere. One of the highlights of the cruise had been sailing past the World Trade Center on our way out to sea.

One thing I did not convey to this acquaintance (but that seemed eerie in retrospect) was something that had occurred on board the ship before we set sail from the West Side cruise ship terminal.

The ETC students and chaperoning faculty had quickly deposited their gear in their staterooms and scurried up on deck to absorb every second of this experience. Everyone in the program is of drinking age, so, beers or cocktails in hand, the students rushed to congregate on the outside deck along with the rest of the ship's passengers, basking in the waning summer sunshine while enjoying the New York skyline.

Around the outdoor pool, we found that a veritable drinking contest had commenced. On one side of the aft deck were New York City firefighters; on the other side were New York City policemen—all off-duty. They were there as civilians eager for respite from their intense urban existence. Uniformed in shorts and T-shirts, suntan lotion and shades, these two contingents of fiercely competitive but complementary guardians of the city had decided to have some fun.

An ETC student, standing beside me watching this display of New York machismo, made a derogatory comment about the public nature of this drinking competition.

"Have you ever lived in New York?" I asked her.

"No," came the reply.

"If you knew what New York City cops and firefighters have to put up with on a daily basis, you would readily and happily forgive the noise, the language, and the pleasure they are having right now. These folks put their lives on the line every day in their jobs. If they want to let loose on a cruise-to-nowhere, I think we should just let them."

Little did I know what these brave public servants would face in just forty-eight hours' time.

The next morning, Sunday, September 9, 2001, we docked again in New York and boarded our bus for the trip back to Pittsburgh. But before departing the city I asked the driver to make a loop of Manhattan while I served as tour guide. That detour took us down West Side Highway, past the World Trade Center. I pointed it out with great pride, as any native New Yorker would do. It was more alive in my mind at that time than ever before. Two days later it was a part of tragic history.

Five years after that, following a relaxing evening at the ballpark and a rare Pirates win, I had shaken off the weightiness of those memories and the cares of the workday. I parked the car in our garage and entered the house to find Jan seated at her desk, looking somewhat distracted and disturbed. After twenty-four years of marriage I know when something is amiss.

Before I could say anything, she said solemnly, "Randy called."

I sensed the weight of bad news in her voice, but never for a minute suspected what she would say next.

"He has been diagnosed with pancreatic cancer."

I just stared at her.

"He wanted to talk to you directly, but when you weren't home he went ahead and told me. He was concerned about how rumors spread like wildfire in circumstances like this, and has decided to send out a group email to everyone. But he wanted to tell you first."

Even in this horrible circumstance, Randy was logical, thorough, and concerned about others. Jan said that he carefully quoted prognosis statistics and repeatedly apologized for delivering such bad news.

Many people report that their lives pass before their eyes when they confront life-threatening circumstances. Trust me then when I claim to have seen at that very moment our entwined lives pass before mine. My head was overloaded with images of our six years together. I recalled Randy's natural aversion to illness, his tremendous zest for life, his arrival in the office after a game of basketball with friends and colleagues from computer science. I thought about the kindness and generosity of spirit Randy had shown to me during my own bout with cancer, his filial love and concern at his father's terminal illness, and his incredible devotion to his wife and children.

Cancer survivors relive their own shock and horror whenever they learn that someone they know has been diagnosed with cancer, the statement "You have cancer" like an all-too-familiar echo in the mind. Cancer brands for life all who experience it.

My thoughts immediately turned from cancer in general to the kind of cancer with which Randy had been diagnosed. There is a definite hierarchy within this disease, and, while all cancers are bad, some are most definitely worse than others. Cancer patients talk among themselves about good cancers and bad cancers. Randy himself would later call Steve Jobs lucky for having the "good" kind of pancreatic cancer—unlike Randy.

There is no doubt about it: Pancreatic cancer is very bad news. It was essentially a death sentence in 2006, and while advances continue to be made in combating the disease, it remains a cancer with a daunting mortality rate.

I absorbed the impact of this news, wondering what I would say to my dear friend when I called him back. Sharing the same physician gave me a foundation on which to begin the discussion, but I knew at some point we would talk about the existential aspects of mortality. When I thought about Randy's family, his three young children and loving, devoted wife, I became near catatonic. It took me awhile to muster the strength to make the call.

When I did connect with Randy that evening, I felt more anxious than he seemed to be. Once again, Randy's ability to apply logic and reason to a highly emotional situation allowed him to speak of his diagnosis with a sense of detachment. He didn't go so far as to speak in third person, but he was definitely a man in command. This was his way of stating that, although his body had turned against him, his mind remained his own. And, with consciousness on his side, could assert his defiance and independence.

I don't recall the specifics of our conversation; shock ruled. The desire to maintain an aura of normalcy in the face of such heinous news confounded much of what I really wanted to say. At times like this, my Catholic religion manifests itself front and center. As the old expression goes, "There are no atheists in a foxhole."

Randy was thrust into a foxhole all right, on the front lines of the biggest battle of his life. How he would react spiritually was a question in the minds of many of his friends.

Randy asked that I keep his news confidential until he had the chance to compose his email revealing it to his friends, colleagues, students, former students, and others.

I intended to honor his request, but the news was so overwhelming that I felt compelled to call our mutual friend and fellow ETC faculty member Jesse Schell. Jesse is the man Randy had asked to replace him in the Building Virtual Worlds class and whose hiring at the ETC Randy had championed. Jesse and I shared our shock in a conversation filled with lots of pauses and "I don't knows." Neither of us doubted for a second that Randy would fight the disease to the end.

On September 12, shortly before high noon, friends and acquaintances of Randy Pausch received an email conveying the devastating news of his pancreatic cancer diagnosis. With typical Randy understatement he referred to this development as "unfortunate news."

He tried to temper the severity of the diagnosis by declaring that he was one of a small percentage of adenocarcinoma patients who qualified for a surgical procedure called the Whipple procedure. There was no getting around the fact that this was serious surgery. It involved removal of the tumor, part of the pancreas, the gallbladder, part of the small intestine, and perhaps even part of the stomach. Once the surgery was complete and he recovered enough, Randy would then commence a grueling regimen of radiation and/ or chemotherapy.

I cringed thinking about the extent of such intervention. Still, Randy possessed an indomitable and positive attitude. He even talked about the potential for full recovery. Reviewing the mathematical odds for pancreatic cancer survival, however, underscored just how daunting a proposition he was confronting. Only 10 to 20 percent of patients undergoing the Whipple procedure lived longer than five years. Randy's spirit and determination, however, gave one the sense that he had every intention of joining that select group.

For a man who tended to react to the common cold with fear and trembling, opting to undergo this procedure could only mean one thing: his newfound life as husband and father was so meaningful and important that he would take any and every step necessary to live as long as possible for his beloved family.

As Randy described the procedure to me, I found myself wondering if I would have the guts to agree to that level of intervention, or if I would accept the inevitable, giving up the possibility of some extra time with my loved ones in order to avoid the pain and discomfort. Would palliative care have won out over such serious intervention? Thankfully, all of this remains conjecture on my part. For Randy the decision was clear.

Always finding the dark humor in a bad situation, I said to Randy, "Gee, I get cancer and now you have to get cancer! But since yours is more of a 'real' cancer, I guess you win."

Immediately Randy replied, "Yeah, but yours is rarer."

"Hmm, then I guess we both win!" I declared triumphantly.

We laughed together. Our shared laughter ended with a sigh.

"That Whipple procedure sure sounds like a major undertaking. My cancer operation was akin to mole removal compared to what you are about to go through. But the folks at the University of Pittsburgh Medical Center were simply terrific."

I could tell Randy was glad to hear that. "Yeah, and I am fortunate in having Dr. Herbert Zeh performing my Whipple; he's performed hundreds of Whipple surgeries. He even gave me his cell phone number and email so I can contact him anytime." Once again, connectivity proved essential to Randy!

I then told him about the time in 1983 when my wife, Jan, was diagnosed with Systemic Lupus Erythematosus. She was serving in the U.S. Army, and as a result of becoming ill while on active duty was hospitalized at Walter Reed Army Hospital in Washington, D.C. I recall distinctly one of the physicians at Walter Reed telling her how lucky she was to live in Pittsburgh. "If you're going to get sick, get sick in Pittsburgh," he said. Randy was very happy to hear further confirmation of UPMC's capabilities and professional renown.

One fellow I felt genuine sympathy for was our dear family practice physician, Dr. Rabinowitz. Between the two of us, we had stretched Dr. Rabinowitz's diagnostic skills: My "almost always benign" parathyroid adenoma turned out to be one of the rarest forms of malignancy, while Randy's "apparent hepatitis" turned out to be pancreatic cancer.

The first time I visited Dr. Rabinowitz after the Last Lecture and resulting media hubbub, I said to him jokingly, "I guess you'll never accept any new patients I might recommend."

He laughed heartily, while vigorously shaking his head. I could see how and why both Randy and I enjoyed and respected Dr. Rabinowitz.

The strain of dark humor between Randy and me continued through the following months. At one point he suggested donating his skull to serve as the ETC's Randy Pausch Award. He joked that it could be passed on from winner to winner, though he feared Jai would nix the idea.

For more than a little while, it seemed as though Randy had indeed triumphed over the cancer. Those halcyon days reached their zenith on May 4, 2007, when Randy announced on his website that he was cancer-free. Having been in that position before, I could empathize with how good that declaration must have felt to him. However, once you've had cancer, you also know that "cancer-free" is a relative term. It means the cancer is at best truly gone or at least in abeyance (not progressed enough to register on scans or inflict detectable damage to the body). It also means "enjoy it while it lasts." And that Randy did.

What followed were some wonderfully heady days during which Randy's zest for life was there in full force. Knowing that this spate of good health was most likely a temporary respite rather than a genuine triumph over pancreatic cancer, Randy created as many memories as possible with his family. Sensing that time was ultimately going to shortchange him, he set about creating a Randy-style "time management regimen" to maximize whatever time he did have remaining.

His amazing endurance following the surgery and chemo resulted in his body staving off a recurrence of the cancer longer than most people had conjectured. Even he admitted that he appeared to be one of the healthiest dying men any of us had ever encountered. He and I joked that if he lived much longer, there could be well-wishers demanding their condolence cards back. All of this made for good laughs in the face of a difficult situation. We both knew deep down that the humor was our attempt at warding off the sadness and horror of the inevitable. I was certain similar banter was occurring between Randy and Steve Seabolt, his best friend from Electronic Arts.

The period between early May and late August 2007 would prove to be the halcyon days for Randy's extended good health. All of us held out the prospect that perhaps he had become one of the few to have actually beaten pancreatic cancer. His quality-of-life effervescence sure made it seem like that might actually be the case.

Consequently, the whole community of Randy's friends and colleagues were stunned on August 26 when Randy sent out an email informing everyone that his cancer had returned, that he should now expect only three to six more months of good health. He also let everyone know that he and his family were planning a move down to Virginia to be closer to Jai's family. He included a link to his website, where he would be posting updates. This website would serve as the primary means through which Randy would communicate with his ever-growing legion of well-wishers.

Reading this email, I could see that Randy's factual, logical approach to how much time he had left on this earth was triumphing over hope. The realization that whatever physical benefit had resulted from the Whipple procedure, the near-fatal chemotherapy, and Randy's optimistic attitude was now at an end and hit all of us hard. There was no doubt he was still a Tigger at heart, but a subdued one for the time being.

Little did we know that instead of retreating into a doom-and-gloom depressive state, Randy was about to embark on an existence so peripatetic and positive that many of us would soon come to feel that by sheer force of will and the cumulative good wishes of the world's citizenry he might yet conquer cancer.

We in the ETC read with admiration—and even a bit of envy—of the non-stop agenda of fun things that Randy and his family were doing following his final diagnosis. Of course we were heartbroken at the news that he and his family were leaving Pittsburgh, doubly so because they had only recently moved back into their home after a major renovation to customize the house perfectly for their family life.

Randy was not attached to material goods—another quality that he and I shared. I have always said one should be able to live out of a car if need be. And, while the ETC—and my office in particular—is crammed with toys, models, posters, photos, baseball bobble heads, and all sorts of other memorabilia, I am prepared to kiss it all good-bye in a heartbeat. It really is just stuff.

Randy's house, though, was his gift to Jai and his children. When I first met him, he invited me over to his "room." He was living on the third floor of the home of Doug Cooper, a professor in the College of Fine Arts. It was a tiny room, more appropriate for a destitute college student than a tenured, albeit bachelor, professor. My initial reaction upon entering this cell was incredulity. Randy had obviously encountered this reaction before and proceeded to offer up an explanation.

"You're probably wondering why I am living in a sparsely furnished third-floor room of a colleague's house," he said, rhetorically.

"The question had crossed my mind," I stuttered.

His answer was concise and to-the-point: "To save money!"

He said then that he knew the day would come when he would need to purchase a house for the woman of his dreams and their inevitable family. When that time came, he wanted to be prepared financially to spare no expense in providing them with their dream house. To know that he'd created his dream home at last, only to put it on the market, was yet another devastating development in the saga of Randy Pausch.

Happily, Randy's friends rallied to his every need. Assistance came forth from former and current students, colleagues, neighbors, and congregation members from the Unitarian Church to which Randy and Jai belonged. All were willing and eager to help the family pack up their house and move to Virginia.

Carnegie Mellon President Jerry Cohon and Computer Science Dean Randy Bryant kindly allocated computer science staff member Cleah Schlueter to assist Randy and Jai full-time with their logistical needs, especially the growing number of inquiries pouring into Randy's website.

Reviewing Randy's website to keep track of the latest medical news while learning of his latest family adventure became an important daily event in the lives of people who knew him, as well as those who didn't. We read with glee of Randy's amazing dolphin swim with his eldest son, Dylan. We looked with disbelief and amazement at photos of Randy scuba diving in the Cayman Islands with his best friends. Randy turned his website into a veritable vicarious-living portal. He did his utmost to share his life with those who were interested—and the number of people interested continued to grow daily.

Questions remained, of course, concerning Randy's ongoing involvement with Carnegie Mellon University. Would he periodically visit campus as long as his health held up, or would the precious time remaining be devoted entirely to his family?

The ever-logistical Randy anticipated and answered that and other questions in the following email to Drew Davidson, Jesse Schell, and me on August 31, 2007:

From: pausch@cs.cmu.edu
Subject: talk at 4:30pm on Tuesday, Sept 18th
Date: August 31, 2007 9:29:35 AM EDT

Messers ETC,

If the dam don't break and the creek don't flood, I'm scheduled to give a talk on Tuesday, Sept 18th at 4:30pm, as part of the University-wide lecture series on "Journeys." (This lecture series *used* to be called "Last Lectures," as in "if you knew you were going to die and had one last lecture to give, what would it be?"—and to think for *once* I really nailed the venue!).

Anyway, since the talk is going to be "Really Achieving One's Childhood Dreams," I thought it might be appropriate for ETCers to attend, since I view the ETC as a factory that we have all created to enable that mission. I realize it's very inconvenient, being on main campus on a BVW day.

It's currently scheduled for the Adamson Wing (Baker Hall 136A), but they are looking into moving it to Wean Hall 7500 or McConomy. Apparently, I'm living the old Disney maxim about scarcity increasing value. . . .

Details:
University Lecture Series
"Really Achieving One's Childhood Dreams," by Randy Pausch
Tuesday, Sept 18th at 4:30pm
Baker Hall 136A (but may move)

Thanks,
Randy

We delighted in knowing that Randy would have one last hurrah, a final opportunity to teach. The actor's dictum "The show must go on!" was alive and well in this computer scientist. He would surely seek to make his final lecture at Carnegie Mellon a performance for the ages, the fulfillment of right-brain/left-brain cohesion. Randy would demonstrate one last time just how to combine entertainment and education.

With his Last Lecture, Randy had a positive impact on more people than any teacher could ever imagine. In becoming a teacher Randy became a procreator of knowledge, and I daresay he manifested the truth that we are all meant to be teachers. Everything we do is the result of what we have learned and what we teach, intentionally or inadvertently. Randy's Last Lecture would be the epitome of that realization. Randy's final performance would underscore how truly effective teaching is the coming together of right-brain and left-brain thinking. The world's reaction would confirm that learning is, fundamentally, the same thing.

Chapter Eleven
The Last Lecture

The Last Lecture had been a traditional part of the Carnegie Mellon educational framework for many years. I know because I gave my Last Lecture way back in 1988.

In hindsight, the fact that I gave a Last Lecture after having been at Carnegie Mellon a mere seven years is a testament to how desperate the Last Lecture folks must have been to find speakers at the time. I think they sought someone who might be entertaining rather than holding out for someone who could offer the genuine insights that were beyond a young whippersnapper like myself at the time.

The notes from my personal Last Lecture have been long since erased from some long-departed hard drive, but I recall using the "All the World's a Stage" metaphor to convey my view of life and education. In what now seems a foreshadowing of my eventual career path, I tried hard to get across the idea that there shouldn't be any bifurcation between the two.

My own experience colored my initial reaction to Randy telling me he had been invited to give the Last Lecture. The gravitas of his situation and the incredible irony inherent in the invitation were shocking. I could not accept the weight of the word "last." Randy liked to talk about the phenomenon of cognitive dissonance. Well, having a conversation in which he calmly informed me that he had only a few months to live created a whopping case of cognitive dissonance in me.

Randy asked if I would be willing to introduce him at the lecture. I said I'd be honored to do so, save for the unfortunate fact that I would be away, on a recently rescheduled major recruitment trip to Taiwan and Singapore with Rebecca Lombardi, the ETC's director of admissions and marketing. The word "rescheduled" here carries some intense frustration. The decision to go global proved a daunting undertaking, but one I believed in fully. Finding suitable windows for international travel while overseeing the workings of the ETC had proven much more difficult than I had ever imagined.

So, I told Randy I thought I'd be in Taiwan on that date—to which he replied, "Well then it is going to be very difficult for you to introduce me."

This was followed by one of those discomfiting pauses that indicate neither person knows what to say next. I know Randy was disappointed. Whether he was disappointed because our schedules just didn't mesh or because he was hoping I would rearrange my schedule to accommodate his request is something we never discussed. Knowing how concerned Randy was that very few people might show up for his Last Lecture makes me think he feared my conflict would be the first of many, resulting in sparse attendance. Or perhaps he was expecting more of me than I was able to deliver emotionally at that time, and my demurral felt like one more let-down.

In hindsight, I realize that allowing myself to be unavailable to introduce Randy at his Last Lecture was another attempt on my part to deny his illness. The deaths of my grandfather and father from cancer, as well as my personal run-in with the disease, have led me to recognize that denial is a coping mechanism. Sadly, this is something usually realized after the fact. Looking back after all that has transpired since the lecture, do I wish that I had been there and done what Randy asked of me? The answer is yes.

It might be hard for the millions of people who have viewed the Last Lecture to believe that Randy feared no one might attend, but it is true. To counter that concern, Randy sent out email invitations to friends, former students, colleagues, associates, and others who had mattered in his life. I admired, yet again, his rational, logical process. He was doing everything possible to ensure there would be an audience for what he intended to be the most important speech of his life.

Prior to my departure I sent Randy the following note:

September 16, 2007

Dear Randy,

I write this just prior to my departure for two weeks in Asia recruiting prospective ETC students in Taiwan, and finalizing an ETC presence in Singapore. I lament not being there for your talk, but am consoled in knowing it will be captured digitally for me and posterity. Given the weird time differential between Asia and the 'Burgh I don't really know where I'll be when it is broadcast live!

A veritable army of Randy Pausch alumni is converging on Pittsburgh from all over the country and I know you will be 'blown away' by this overt and outward expression of respect, honor, and 'flat out' love.

So to you, partner, I send along the fondest wish any actor can extend to another: Break a Leg! It means literally for one to put on a show that is so magnificent and makes such an impact upon an audience that one's bow is not only genuine and well-deserved, but serves as a gift given back to those in attendance for their presence, attention, dedication, and gratitude.

Break a Leg!
Don

When Jeff Zaslow and I first spoke over the telephone afterward, he asked me what I thought of Randy's Last Lecture, and if I had ever seen anything as spectacular in my life. I told him that I thought Randy had hit the ball out of the park and had given the best lecture of his life, precisely because it mattered so much to him. As Randy himself had put it, he finally "nailed the venue!" This was a make-or-break moment, and Randy was not to be denied.

When Jeff asked me if I had heard the stories, tales, and words of wisdom imparted that day, I replied, "of course," because I surely had. I'd have to say that 80 percent of the Last Lecture was made up of stories I had heard before. But that in no way detracted from the impact of what Randy had said. His wisdom had been forged in the furnace of life experience. The unique portions of the Last Lecture were his thoughts and feelings about Jai, Dylan, Logan, and Chloe, along with a few other "true confession" moments that stunned me.

One aspect of the talk that was new to me was Randy's metaphor about brick walls. I had never heard him use this particular turn of phrase before, though the analogy was consistent with the Randy I had known. Brick walls are the obstacles, the antagonists (as we say in the theater), preventing us from realizing our dreams. Our ability to overcome them is directly proportional to our desire to achieve our goal. Randy had created a beautiful metaphor that resonated with listeners; brick walls have become an onerous aspect of everyday life for most people. Instead of inhibiting our motivation, however, these brick walls can enhance it. Randy was not about to let the brick wall of pancreatic cancer inhibit his making an impact on the world. After listening to Randy's Last Lecture, I'm sure people everywhere contemplated the degree to which they had become brick walls to others; likewise the degree to which brick walls had gotten the better of them, winning out over daring and perseverance.

The day of Randy's Last Lecture, I was winging my way over the Pacific Ocean, heading for Taiwan and a whirlwind few days of speaking engagements, recruitment sessions, and meetings with potential colleagues and collaborators. The Singapore Airlines jet began its descent into Taipei as I awoke from the one hour of fitful sleep I had managed on the fourteen-hour flight. The intercom crackled with the voice of the pilot, who spewed a rapid succession of words all containing the prefix "tai." It never registered that we were descending amidst a *typhoon* currently hitting *Taipei, Taiwan*, until the aircraft took on the movements of a roller coaster. Trust me when I say this was one moment I regretted not remaining in Pittsburgh to attend the Last Lecture!

One white-knuckled landing later, I found myself confronting belligerent taxi drivers in my quest to get to my downtown hotel. "Don't you know there's a typhoon happening?" one of them shouted as I threw my bags into his trunk.

Pointing to my ashen fellow passengers, I replied, "Oh yes, I am well aware of it. Now let's go."

We were among very few cars on the road and managed to make it into downtown Taipei in record time. The desk clerk at the hotel informed me that it probably wouldn't be wise to walk the streets of Taipei in search of a restaurant; anyway, they were all closed due to the storm. Wondering exactly how dumb I looked, I assured her that tonight's dinner was going to be room service.

"Do you have high-speed Internet?" was all I was really interested in. I intended to spend the evening in my room watching Randy's Last Lecture. She assured me the hotel's Internet was indeed still working.

Concerned about timing and connectivity, I recall plopping my bags down and immediately setting up my laptop. I accessed the URL and, lo and behold, there was Randy on the screen.

Along with everyone watching in McConomy Auditorium, or on the screens in the adjoining rooms of the Carnegie Mellon University Center, I was spellbound as my cofounder and suite-mate of six years commenced the lecture of a lifetime.

The first thing that struck me was the humility that came forth when Randy hushed the crowd by telling them, "Make me earn it." I knew then and there that this was not going to be simply one more public performance by the most versatile and engaging computer scientist I had ever met. I knew that Randy was raising the stakes.

Then he hit the floor and started doing push-ups, and I just shook my head in wonder. Randy was as concretely inclined as I am. Rather than talk about the cognitive dissonance between his current state and his death sentence he set out to *show* us!

When he chastised anyone inclined to pity him, though, I sensed the arrogance and acrimony that he could also project. Pity, in and of itself, is not necessarily a bad thing. Those of us in the theater have long accepted Aristotle's admonition to create tragic characters specifically capable of eliciting the feeling of pity (as well as fear) in audiences. Pity, though, involves emotion; and emotions and Randy were rather akin to fire and water. He tended to avoid or undercut them with reason and logic.

Randy's Last Lecture followed a much more linear narrative than I imagined it would, though I did expect him to emphasize the journey of his life to date. I listened intently to what he had to say, but, in all honesty, I listened even more carefully to how he said it. His resolve, his control, his rhythm and cadence were vintage Randy. He was in control and in command.

Naturally, I was eager to hear how he would describe the establishment of the ETC, and curious about how time, distance, circumstance, and expectation would affect his recollection. I was therefore rather stunned when I saw a photograph of me that I had never seen before, projected onto the McConomy screen. It was one of the least flattering photos of me ever taken. Even I had to peer closely at the image to make sure it was me on the screen and not a cartoon caricature. I appeared almost dwarflike, leering at a woman in a black evening dress, my eyes bulging. I was wearing my then-signature straw hat. From more than seven thousand miles away, I could hear the McConomy audience chuckling at the image.

The truth is, I wasn't laughing. I have always hated looking at photographs of myself. My self-image has never matched what I see in the mirror. They say a photograph adds ten pounds; well, I have always thought it more like a hundred pounds.

The next photo showed the two of us dressed as a rock-and-roll guitarist (me) and the quintessential nerd (him). He laughed at that one (as he always did) and credited me with thinking up the pose (which was true). Whatever disappointment I had felt just seconds before vanished as I thought back to the time the second photo was taken and the fun we had playing up the notion of an artsy creative type and a classic geek with pocket-protector, white lab coat, and horn-rimmed glasses.

I was absorbed in Randy's recollections of the ETC's origins. I was flattered beyond belief when he publically credited me with having done 70 percent of the work to make the ETC what it had become. I knew he was referring to the logistical structure of the place, because the educational mission was entirely an equal undertaking. Randy's generosity of spirit was welcome and heartwarming.

This warm and fuzzy feeling waned again when, leaning against the podium sporting a Cheshire-cat grin, Randy quipped about his six years of sharing an office with yours truly. "Someone asked me, 'Given your current condition, have you thought about whether you're going to go to heaven or hell?' And I said, 'I don't know, but if I'm going to hell I'm getting six years for time served.'"

The auditorium rocked with laughter. I was perplexed. Randy and I had challenged each other regularly during our time together, but I would never have classified it as *hellish*. Maybe that's because our definitions of "conflict" came from very different places.

He then bestowed on me the honorific in the title of this book. "Sharing an office with Don was really like sharing an office with a tornado. There was just so much energy, and you never knew which trailer was next, but you knew something exciting was going to happen . . . Don is an intense guy . . . Don is crazy, but I mean that in a good way."

I knew he meant that in a good way; I just wondered if everyone else listening understood it in a good way. Would they understand that the "trailers" Randy credited me with confronting were the closed minds of arrogance, lack of imagination, the easy-way-out, inefficient use of resources, bad habits, sloth, unproductive routines, waste, rash decisions, ignorance, fear, bias, prejudice, and myriad other obstacles, almost all of human creation. That, in fact, we were both seeking to confront those "trailers"?

Randy prefaced his recollection of our time together by stating that he knew I would forgive his generating humor at my expense. Sadly, he was giving me more credit than I deserved at that moment. I'm known as a king of sarcasm, but it is tough sometimes to take what one can so readily dish out. His comments about me during the Last Lecture had me swaying like a pendulum between hurt feelings and immense honor. I was very happy, therefore, when he moved on to discuss his first love, Alice, and the true loves of his life: Jai and the children.

It was at this point that the immensity of the Last Lecture truly resonated. This autobiographical recollection referencing technologies and academic institutions revealed that the true power behind creativity is *love*. Randy showed that love is what you do. He said he did the Last Lecture for his wife and children. That was only half true, in my opinion. I think he did the Last Lecture for all of us.

The depth of Randy's transformation into the true embodiment of right-brain/left-brain thinking would not manifest itself until Carnegie Mellon's 2008 commencement ceremony. It was then and there that the true power within each of us to change the world was revealed.

At the beginning of the Last Lecture, Randy responded to the ovation he received by advising the audience to make him "earn it." He showed during that spellbinding hour and a half precisely what he meant by that. Most of us in education are aware of Thomas Alva Edison's famous quote: "Success is 10 percent inspiration and 90 percent perspiration." What Randy did was add the secret ingredient of joy.

Chapter Twelve

The Comet Lights Up the Sky

No one—and I mean *no one*—foresaw the media explosion that radiated from the Last Lecture. Credit a combination of old and new media. Jeff Zaslow's series of articles in the *Wall Street Journal* represented traditional journalism at its best, but a more recent media outlet, YouTube, was the TNT that blasted the Last Lecture around the world.

The global fallout of the Last Lecture video confirmed for any skeptical mind the true power of the Internet's viral capabilities. Once the Last Lecture became available via YouTube, it tapped into the massive social network of the prime demographic for its message. The Internet has allowed word-of-mouth—the most powerful form of promotion in existence—to evolve into text-based interaction. As more and more people watched the Last Lecture on YouTube, they telephoned, emailed, texted, and chatted online and in person to alert friends and family of its existence. What resulted was a positive pandemic of excitement, appreciation, and utter amazement.

It is generally agreed that viral distribution alone cannot sustain a major marketing thrust. Carnegie Mellon alumnus Jeff Zaslow must be recognized for bringing Randy's Last Lecture to the attention of readers of traditional media. (The truth is, almost all of us in the ETC missed the original *Wall Street Journal* feature and had to be alerted to it via forwarded emails.) On Sunday, April 6, 2008, Randy appeared on the cover of *Parade* magazine, a well-known national publication, and in the *Orlando Sentinel*. This was followed in rapid succession by stories in *The New York Times*, the London *Times*, *Reader's Digest*, the cover of *USA Today*'s "Life" section, and numerous Associated Press articles in other publications.

The flame ignited by traditional print media became a firestorm of interest once the broadcast media picked up the story. Everyone was eager to find out more about Randy, his amazing Last Lecture, and the ensuing world reaction. His story was featured on *Good Morning America*, the *CBS Evening News*, *20/20*, *Oprah*, and *The Ellen DeGeneres Show*. The newscaster who would prove to be the most simpatico with Randy and his plight was ABC's Diane Sawyer, who hosted a popular prime-time special about him.

The buzz over the Last Lecture continued unabated for months. From the live Internet feed through the YouTube posting, periodicals, and television, the story was the talk at every watercooler. The world was hungry for more information, and it was inevitable that the publishing world would enter the arena.

Jeff Zaslow's column ignited the interest of traditional publishers in bringing Randy's story and message to people in book form. Until the Last Lecture, publishers weren't very savvy about mining YouTube videos as a source for potential best sellers. I would venture to say that has changed, thanks to Randy. There are probably stringers all over the country nowadays searching YouTube for potential book and movie ideas.

Randy alerted me via email of Jeff Zaslow's intention to write a book. He advised me that I should feel free to have as much or as little contact with Jeff as I desired. Jeff was a Carnegie Mellon alumnus and a distinguished author in his own right, so there was no doubt whatsoever in my mind that I would be as forthcoming as possible with stories, anecdotes, accounts, and myriad remembrances of our time together. I inundated Jeff with tales and recollections that brought many a smile to my face. My, how time had flown, and what vicissitudes of experiences we both had undergone.

Randy and I remained in touch by email during this time. Knowing Randy's penchant for time management I figured there was very little time in his day for idle chatter. One could say that email served as our form of text messaging. It was something we could do when and where we felt like. I tried not to be an imposition on his time. The ever-growing activities of the ETC and global travel served to limit my own free time for socializing and communication.

Telephone calls and emails started coming to me through the ETC almost immediately after the Last Lecture appeared on YouTube, and became even more frenzied once the traditional media spread the news across multiple demographics. I was extremely touched by those messages expressing or soliciting empathy. For every sympathetic message there was another asking Randy to speak to a relative or loved one also suffering from terminal illness.

The frenzy was beyond anything the ETC had ever experienced. Many of the telephone calls and emails were from people interested in getting copies of the text of the Last Lecture for friends and family. Others had their own motivations for reaching out, some of which created serious ethical problems for me.

The most bizarre and problematic communiqués came from individuals desperate to reach Randy with pancreatic cancer cures. There were more of these than you might imagine, well-wishers who genuinely believed in the power of a particular medicine, herbal remedy, surgery, or healing power. One writer offered to undergo surrogate surgery for Randy; another directed him to a variety of meditation websites; still others provided elaborate recipes of herbal ingredients.

Some of the correspondence was so powerful it took my breath away, leaving me shaking my head and walking the halls wondering what to do:

> Years ago I discovered the causes of pancreatic cancer and a treatment routine that brings rapid recovery to the patient because it deals with the specific causes at hand. I have never published my findings due to the politics of medicine and my lack of affiliation with some prestigious institution.

> Unfortunately your physicians are doing everything wrong on your behalf. If you and I can discuss the matter on the phone I will explain the underlying causes and why your medical routine is completely wrong. It will totally make sense to you. As you well know, "knowledge is power." You really deserve to have this knowledge before you let your doctors continue with their disastrous medical routine. Then the decision is yours to make.

Randy took these messages in stride. His retort to one of them left me laughing hysterically. He simply marveled at how someone could claim to know the cure for cancer but not think of using the Internet to find his email address. The quip was so typically Randy that I thought for a minute he had been cured and was his old self again.

Many other calls and emails were spiritual in nature, offering prayers for Randy and his family, urging conversion (on the presumption that Randy was without faith), or calling upon extrasensory or otherworldly intervention. These left me unsure how to respond. One came from a college student concerned about the absence of God in all of Randy's presentations. Here's the gist:

> I was inspired by you not because of what you said, but because of what you didn't say. I believe and know to be true that there is a God, your creator, who is capable of healing. He can heal you from cancer completely if he wants to. In fact, he can do anything he wants. Do you believe that he wants to do this for you? He does! Let it be done to you according to your faith in Him. Just ask him and be persistent . . .

> What have you to lose? Your past doesn't matter anymore; your beliefs don't even matter anymore. This is about you making a conscious decision to submit to God's authority.

I knew Randy well enough to know that he wouldn't appreciate such sentiments, though I couldn't exactly pinpoint the reasons religious discussions were so problematic for him. After a lot of reflection, I decided that the only responsible thing to do was pass the inquiries on to Randy. What he did with them was entirely his decision.

Oddly enough, a number of the emails I received were specifically for me. I was extremely touched by one I received from India shortly after Randy died:

> Dear Don,
> This was the only way of reaching out to you, even though you do

not know me. I've just picked up a copy of The Last Lecture and have summoned the courage to read it. It is so ironic, the day I got the link to YouTube, my mother was diagnosed with pancreatic cancer, on the day she was undergoing a biopsy, which resulted in various complications, we learnt through Indian newspapers of Randy's demise (Mum is recovering). You are lucky to have known him in person. He left a lasting legacy behind—his book. Just had to reach out to someone who knew him and say, his book is invaluable.

People were so eager to get messages to Randy that many sought out my home telephone number. My ETC travel schedule remained as intense as ever during this time, so my wife was the one who fielded most of those calls. I came home to an exasperated spouse more than a couple of times, who entertained me with tales of people eager to get through to Randy. Ever sensitive to others, Randy sent apologies to my wife, Jan, for the incursion that the Last Lecture was making into our home life. He was especially sensitive to the letters and phone calls replete with elaborate herbal remedies or exhortations to conversion and higher powers.

One of these home telephone calls was from a zealous Hollywood producer, eager to turn Randy's story into a movie. This wasn't just a vague idea. The producer was ready to go into production, and regaled Jan for almost an hour with a list of current young hunks who would be "perfect" to play Randy. In a sign of our age and lifestyle, my wife didn't recognize a single one of the names he mentioned. Nor did I!

When the possibility of a movie made it into the collective ether of the ETC, the students had some fun positing various casting scenarios. The Schwarzenegger/DeVito combo gave way to other pairings, mainly of stars whose names did not resonate with me. I found myself suggesting to puzzled students that perhaps I could portray myself—I was, after all, an actor.

As of this writing, no movie plans have been finalized, and that might be just as well. Randy conveyed his own message of living life to the fullest so succinctly and well in the Last Lecture and various media interviews that it would be hard to top with a dramatization. And, as he said on the Diane Sawyer ABC special, no one could make a movie of his life because there was no actress beautiful enough to play his wife, Jai. It would be hard for any screenwriter or actor to top that as a tribute to the love of his life.

Randy was focused on the importance of his legacy not for his own exaltation but for the good of those he would be leaving behind. He was often asked what he considered to be his greatest legacy. His answer, both in public interviews and in the book of the Last Lecture, was the creation and dissemination of the Alice software, which helps young people learn programming through storytelling. Storytelling might never have been a key factor in his work were it not for Randy's residency at Disney, his experiences in the Building Virtual Worlds class, and his position at Carnegie Mellon, where the renown of the computer science department was matched by the prestige and historical significance of the drama school.

A side note: There was one inadvertent habit I had pertaining to Alice that drove Randy crazy. I spelled Alice in all capital letters. For some reason I figured the program needed to be differentiated clearly from the book title *Alice in Wonderland*. This drove Randy mad.

"Why do you keep capitalizing Alice?" he would ask, clearly perturbed.

"I don't know," I'd reply. "I guess because I think it's something really BIG."

He would shake his head.

When Randy first got sick and our correspondence was a mix of light and dark humor, I asked him if there was anything I could do for him. "Yes," he answered, "Stop capitalizing Alice." I never did it again.

I was intent that Randy's legacy within the ETC would remain profound and ongoing. Happily, he and I were able to discuss possibilities for remembrances and memorials, though I admitted to having mixed feelings about the topic. I daresay he was more at ease discussing these possibilities than I was.

Even though Randy professed in the Last Lecture that I had done the bulk of the work creating the ETC, attempting to live up to our mutual aspirations is what drove me. I was trying to fulfill our shared aspiration. Randy and I sought to create an educational environment where student dreams could be nurtured and realized. That wasn't just my dream—it was our dream, our shared vision.

As a sign of my appreciation and gratitude for all Randy had done for me personally, his tremendous generosity in sharing his enthusiasm with students, and with being the most personable computer scientist I had ever met, I decided to name the primary ETC classroom and gathering place as the "Randy Pausch Interdisciplinary Studio."

This would be denoted with a brushed aluminum sign adorned with LED technology so that it forever glowed in the ETC purple and green colors. I sent pictures of the sign to Randy on July 19, 2008, and asked him to come to Pittsburgh to christen the room personally. Randy replied to my email with genuine, heartfelt appreciation.

He thanked me.

He also called me "Sir."

I suddenly felt old. I also felt that he was saying good-bye.

Sadly, this would be the last correspondence he and I had.

I then headed off to Osaka, Japan, for discussions with various Japanese officials about the ETC. I landed at Chicago's O'Hare Airport the morning of July 25. Rebecca Lombardi and I had no sooner passed through customs when she received a text message from the ETC informing us that Randy had died that morning. She had the sad, unenviable task of informing me.

My cell phone had a text from Steve Seabolt, Randy's dear friend from Electronic Arts, asking me to call him ASAP. Steve had been at Randy's side when he died. It was commiseration time. Steve and I discussed the wonder of Randy's journey and the harsh reality and finality of his death—although Randy's passing was in no way final because he left so much behind and had such a great impact on the world.

As "Comet Pausch" succeeded in lighting up the skies with his blazing presence, Randy also succeeded in illuminating the power of the Internet in a brand-new way. Shortly after Randy's death, Alexis Madrigal wrote an amazing reflection for *WIRED* magazine about the phenomenon Randy became. She described what has come to be called the "distributed funeral." This is a take on "distributed computing," a means of connecting users and resources in a transparent, open, and scalable way. What she meant was that the Internet had become the locus for expressions of sorrow and a sense of shared mourning. There have been many instances of national mourning—for John F. Kennedy, Robert Kennedy, Martin Luther King Jr., and others—but they didn't have the benefit of instant connectivity and the creation of a virtual community of mourners all over the world.

As news spread of Randy's passing, the Internet lit up with tens of thousands of tweets and blog posts. Google even added a brief tribute on its main search page. But most fascinating and moving were the grief-stricken comments that ran for pages after every obituary or blog post bearing his name. This massive outpouring of grief is now inscribed across all media silos and geographies, respecting no particular corporate or institutional demarcations. There is no official place for expressing sorrow for Randy, no one in charge of the mourning. The Internet has begun to alter one of our deepest and oldest traditions: how we grieve and with whom we share our sense of loss.

The mourning for Randy served as a kind of bookend for the experience of hearing him speak via the Internet. People had interacted with Randy through a little window embedded in a Web page. Headphones delivered his nuggets of wisdom directly. He seemed to be talking to each person individually, not hundreds packed into a theater or gathered around a television. In response, then, it made sense to reach out personally and say, "Thanks, Randy. We'll miss you."

The strength of the Internet community's reaction to the medium's most famous death-defying cancer patient shows how the Internet has come of age, not just as a market or means of distribution but as a series of linked communities significant enough to seek and exchange affirmations in the face of death.

What Randy Pausch was really a part of—in both his life and his death—was the transformation of virtual reality into a fully functioning parallel universe as real as corporeal existence (if not more so). Randy helped us answer the question, "If we build a parallel universe with attributes normally associated with surreal existence, will they come?" Thanks in part to Randy, the answer is a resounding yes, albeit one spoken through tears.

Chapter Thirteen
All You Need Is Love

One of the requisites of great stories with universal appeal is that the hero undergoes a transformation as a result of his or her journey. The idea that one could go through a major adventure such as success, failure, war, marriage, childbearing, or death, and remain the same person is antithetical to everything we believe about great stories—or life itself, for that matter.

Dorothy in *The Wizard of Oz* exemplifies this kind of transformation. In the course of the story, she changes from a young girl running away from the family farm because no one understands her, into a young woman who finds joy in the realization that there is "no place like home." Her change is brought about by an elaborate allegorical dream triggered by a conk on the head during a (you guessed it) tornado. The Last Lecture has had the tremendous impact it has precisely because it has acted as a transformative "conk on the head" for millions of viewers and readers.

The publicity surrounding the Last Lecture and Randy's subsequent passing resulted in my receiving numerous emails and telephone calls from former classmates. People I hadn't seen in decades contacted me to express condolences and touch base. They were motivated no doubt by the generosity of Randy's spirit and the example he set of expressing his innermost feelings publicly and repeatedly. They took to heart his insistence that we should not wait to express our love, affection, and gratitude. Time management took on a whole new meaning: We never really know how much time we have.

Some of the expressions of sorrow were uplifting in their praise and accolades. Ben Noel, the executive director of the University of Central Florida's Interactive Entertainment Academy, honored us greatly when he wrote: "Randy took a bad situation and made it grand . . . Randy-style. FIEA is here because of people like you and Randy, and places like the ETC."

Kirk Martini, an associate professor of Architecture at the University of Virginia and a colleague of Randy's at UVA, sent me a very touching email after Randy died. It was insightful because it revealed the artist and dramatist I had often glimpsed in my codirector:

> You said that in a great story, the hero is always transformed. I think the thing that transformed Randy most in his professional work is that he came to appreciate the power of storytelling. That arose from his experience at Disney, and working with you at the ETC. I could see in the older Randy a deep understanding that the technology's primary purpose was to support the telling of stories. His grasp of that power is part of what propelled the Last Lecture around the world.

I also received a condolence note from Randy Hinrichs, a dear friend of Randy's and mine from Microsoft who was one of the first to believe in the vision of the ETC:

> Randy's family is surely stricken with unknowing grief by Randy's passing. I didn't know his family, but I know you. You are/were his other family. The family of two. Sharing the same breathing space, spending the best part of the day together, cavorting in brilliant design and wonderful accomplishments. So, I am imagining, even feeling from 3,000 miles away, your own personal grief. My heart goes out to you, and of course to all of those who knew Randy. But, Don, I especially know how hard this has hit you too.

For those of us who knew and worked with Randy Pausch, there is no doubt whatsoever that he underwent fundamental change during his battle with pancreatic cancer. That battle was more than medical, more than physical. It was as fundamental as asking the meaning of life. Many of us knew Randy as a renowned professor, we observed the joie de vivre of his bachelorhood, we marveled at his intense courtship of Jai, we were joyous at their marriage, and we stood in awe as Randy embraced fatherhood and developed into super-family-man.

In a discussion with ETC faculty members Ralph Vituccio and Scott Stevens, Randy was once asked about his legacy. His answer was intriguing. He said he had hoped originally that it would be the creation of the Alice software, but he hoped that in the end he would be known as someone who truly died with dignity.

With this in mind, it is incumbent on us to comprehend and appreciate the journey that took Randy from star athlete, dashing young man, arrogant grad student, and renowned professor, to a fervent proponent of unconditional love and the ultimate importance of family.

For those drawn to Randy's story for reasons they don't fully understand, I suggest it is a subconscious recognition of the journey that Randy, the overt left-brainer, traveled in order to come into full communion with Randy, the closet right-brainer. This transformation saw Randy emerge from the chrysalis of physical decay into a person as whole and actualized as we could wish to encounter in our world today. Randy's example of how to die instead became for millions a model for how to live.

Let us start where we will end up—with *love*. "Love" was not a word the pre-Jai/Dylan/Logan/Chloe Randy uttered very often, at least not in the context it would come to occupy. Granted, Randy always encouraged his students to love their work. Once Jai entered his life, however, the word love resonated in ways it never had before. When Dylan, Logan, and Chloe were born, Randy's love increased exponentially. The ETC's very own Mr. Spock turned into a doting, loving parent who expressed familial and spousal adoration in ways that would have turned romantic poets green with envy.

In my estimation, the most provocative and important statement Randy made during his battle with cancer was made not during his Last Lecture, but rather when he spoke at the 2008 Carnegie Mellon graduation ceremony. At the end of his brief charge to the graduating class, he confessed that he waited so long—until he was 39—to get married because that's how long it took for him to meet the person whose happiness meant more to him than his own. Then, he wished for the same sort of love and passion to be found by each and every one of the graduates.

It was a remarkable confession. It is a statement of truth and wisdom that alone constitutes enough self-realization to justify a life well lived, and humanity well served. This was Randy's way of telling us that we *need* to live for others, that living solely for the self is a dead end. Coming from a self-professed "arrogant professor," this resonated as a powerful message.

Randy's journey saw arrogance transformed into humility. The stark logistics of time management were converted into a quest for and commitment to quality time. He ascribed the value of time to the variable of loving. I chuckle now at how Randy shied away from the hugging and physical contact displayed by theater folk, because it is just about impossible to find a photograph of Randy and his family in which he is not tightly holding onto Jai or the kids. He used the entirety of the senses to imprint memories onto his children. That is precisely what attracts and amazes me about the technology of interactive digital media. It possesses deity-like qualities crafted by humankind in emulation of the creator. This is why I view technology as art.

I love trains. So much so that people inquire as to the source of this obsession. Some of my earliest memories are of my mother holding onto me tightly as we sat on the porch of our home on 15th Avenue in Brooklyn. I would look up at the elevated subway trains, waiting for my father to come home. My mother would sing to me. Ever since that time, I can't look at a train without feeling my mother's arms around me. I can't sit in the womb of a sleeping compartment without feeling as though I am being rocked in a cradle. Everyone I meet on a train, be it in the diner, the club car, or the adjacent seat or compartment, is someone on a journey. It is seldom a rushed journey, so we are provided ample time to contemplate where we are going and why. It is the most *artistic* way to travel.

Randy's most enduring legacy, in my opinion, is that he showed us that true love is the coming together of the qualities and attributes manifest in both halves of our brain. The public never saw logical, rational Randy making sure his family would be cared for after he was gone. They may not appreciate the immense research he undertook to find possible therapies to prolong his life even a little bit. His greatest algorithm was the planning he engaged in for the physical and mental well-being of his family. While the success of the Last Lecture made this easier in many respects, this goal had been with him throughout all his days as a frugal bachelor professor, saving up for the proper partner. In embracing his right-brain qualities, Randy unleashed the love contained therein and facilitated his transformation into a successful provider, a loving, responsible, prescient spouse and parent, and a caring, giving teacher and citizen.

Artists are motivated by love, possibly to the detriment of their left-brain qualities. Randy achieved the crossover. He morphed from being a good-looking and personable "geek" into a superior actor possessing pinnacle skills of emulation and empathy. Doing so, he climbed to the summit of what it means to be fully human, which is what any actor aspires to do. (At Carnegie Mellon we liken the pursuit of a career in theater to a religious vocation. That is how seriously we view the profession of acting.)

Randy achieved what all parents, teachers, leaders, great actors (and saints) aspire to: He became a worthy role model. In doing so, he defined the yin and yang of Western culture as the coming together of right-brain and left-brain thinking. He wound up as the role model for whole-brain thinking, and in the process confirmed that love makes us whole.

Love is also something Randy inspired in the many people who met and worked with him. At his memorial service, I had the pleasure of meeting a former classmate of his who had named her child after Randy. That is a true sign of respect and honor.

Above the proscenium arch of the Kresge Theater in Carnegie Mellon's historic College of Fine Arts is an inscription in French: *Ici l'Inspiration Deploye Ses Ailes*, which means *Here Inspiration Spreads Its Wings*. This saying embodies the aspiration of an enlightened actor transformed willingly into another being before a soon-to-be-enlightened audience. Achieve this and you have reached the theatrical promised land. Randy's personal transformation lights the way to our own transcendence. There really is no greater description of a life well lived.

Epilogue

A Tornado in Search of Trailers

In Kissimmee, Florida, is an amazing wonderland called Give Kids the World. Its origins can be traced to a Nazi concentration camp where a young man by the name of Henri Landwirth vowed to create the exact antithesis of what he was experiencing. He saw children striving to survive while surrounded by death. He subsequently vowed to create a place teeming with life, vitality, imagination, wonderment, and hope for sick and dying children. Mr. Landwirth created an Oz for ill Dorothys.

Every stay includes complimentary VIP visits to the theme parks of Orlando. Children celebrate their birthday no matter what the actual date happens to be. They experience the joy of Christmas. They get to interact with their favorite cartoon characters. They are allowed to eat all the ice cream they want.

The ETC has undertaken various projects for Give Kids the World, providing a variety of entertainment technologies to further enhance the experience. Every ETC student who has ever worked on a Give Kids the World project has considered it life-changing, life-enlightening, and life-enhancing.

Randy and I agreed that we would consider our lives blessed if we could create a *learning* environment of similar vitality. I believe we have come very close to fulfilling that aspiration. The ETC shares much in common with Give Kids the World.

Randy's story about his parents allowing him to paint his bedroom any way he wanted as a child resonates in the physical environment of the

ETC facility. (The fact that so many parents need to be told to let their kids paint their bedrooms really bothers me. My own childhood bedroom was a 1960s psychedelic paradise, my oasis amidst the turmoil of the era. Thank you, Mom and Dad.) Described variously as Carnegie Mellon's Disneyland or an academic version of Willy Wonka's chocolate factory, the ETC has an extravagant decor and color scheme that signify the triumph of creativity and freedom over uniformity and restriction. We have transformed the hospital-like environment of most schools and institutions into one more closely resembling a child's playroom. The result has been liberating beyond words.

The ETC is visited frequently by fellow academics eager to learn the secrets of putting right-brain and left-brain thinkers together. They seek to create similar synergies, and many are taken aback when the first thing I ask them is, "Are you allowed to paint the walls of your building?" If they answer no, I tell them that is precisely the kind of brick wall Randy was talking about. In the same way that the full spectrum of color in a rainbow combines to make white light, the multicolored ETC walls encompass one shared purpose, much like Henry Landwirth's mission at Give Kids the World.

I found my own Henri Landwirth in my dear friend and colleague Anne Humphreys. Anne was one of the first people to contact me when I was diagnosed with parathyroid cancer in 2001. And she didn't just contact me—she tracked me down, set up an off-campus rendezvous at a local coffeehouse, and brought with her many books about dealing with cancer and the life changes that diagnosis brings. This was at the point when my prognosis was still unclear: Maybe I was cured, maybe not.

I was humbled by Anne's generosity of spirit and her desire to share with me her own trials and tribulations with cancer. Anne and I met on and off throughout the first year of my diagnosis. Once a regimen of care had been decided upon for me, Anne felt secure enough to detach herself a bit, but she continued to check in with me regularly to make sure I was doing well physically and mentally.

I considered Anne to be a pioneer in the area of "edutainment," the use of interactive media for educational purposes. Her alignment with the mission of the ETC led to her joining the faculty right about the time Randy was diagnosed with pancreatic cancer. She offered Randy the same level of support she had provided to me during my dark hours. She embodied the suffering Randy was enduring at the same time.

Anne had been afflicted with breast cancer for more than a decade, long before either Randy or I confronted the malady. She had beaten it into submission twice before, but now a third bout with the disease loomed. Even so, her spirit remained indomitable, although the mental and physical struggles were debilitating.

There is something very meaningful and important in Anne's struggle, especially in light of Randy's amazing worldwide fame and influence. In one year within the ETC, two faculty members were stricken with mortal illnesses. Both fought to the very end. Randy transcended his death sentence in one of the most life-affirming manners ever achieved; Anne's battle more closely resembled the quiet and earnest struggle of most individuals afflicted with cancer. Both showed that cancer cannot conquer love.

When Anne died on December 2, 2008, it closed a sorrowful chapter in the story of the ETC. The program had lost two amazing teachers in the same year. One of them became a symbol of hope throughout the world; the other remained a symbol of faith to her family, friends, and colleagues. Although their final journeys were different, their impact on those who knew them was equally profound. They each left new life and invigorated spirits in their wake. They increased the resolve of all those they touched to live more fully than ever before.

Anne never penned a closing statement or a best seller, but she exerted her own kind of influence on the world. Her memorial service was the culmination of a very sad year for the ETC. I feel, in a way, that the world cried as much for Anne as it did for Randy; I know we did in the ETC.

Not too long ago, my wife and I were having dinner at a popular chain restaurant in Pittsburgh. I was wearing my ETC polo shirt with our purple logo emblazoned on the front. I couldn't help but notice the waiter glancing repeatedly at it. During his recitation of the featured dishes, he suddenly stopped and said, "Excuse me, but did you know Randy Pausch?" I nodded, having been asked this many times since the Last Lecture, and commenced explaining how Randy and I cofounded the ETC. As I was talking, the light dawned in his eyes and he exclaimed, "Oh wow, you're the guy who made his life a living hell for six years!" That was definitely not the way to win a big tip, but even I found myself grinning from ear to ear.

Like the comment about hell, other Last Lecture appellations have become indelibly imprinted. As I was checking into a hotel in Bradenton, Florida, during a visit to Pirates spring training together with a team of ETC students, the front desk clerk noticed I worked at Carnegie Mellon. "Did you know the professor who gave the Last Lecture?" she asked excitedly.

"Yes, I did," I responded. "He and I created the Entertainment Technology Center together."

Her jaw dropped. "So you're the crazy guy!"

"Yeah, that's me," I agreed, while my students nodded.

I have become used to these encounters, and have reflected on them. Existential philosophy makes a valid point about our being defined by the "other." In this respect, Randy has done me a great service. Randy's "definitions" have challenged me to look at myself and at how the world perceives me. The initial sting of his descriptions have been tempered by my realization that he hit the nail on the head about our interpersonal dynamic and the way it fueled the creativity of the ETC. I concede that everything he said about me is true—and I take it all as a compliment.

My gravest concern is whether the "can do" philosophy that gave rise to ETC in 1998 even exists today. As a society, we have become terribly risk-averse, allowing ourselves to become dominated by rules and regulations that restrict freedom and imagination. I fear there will eventually be a tax on dreaming! You can't cross a university campus nowadays without tripping over lawyers and auditors. Squelching freedom is not the answer. Rather, we need to reunite freedom and responsibility.

From a meteorological perspective, what is happening is rather clear: a severe cold front is moving in. A preponderance of calculated left-brain thinking is settling over the academic landscape. A misguidance of logic and reason in the form of over-regulation has brought with it the stifling of innovation, risk-taking, and natural inquiry. Imbalance is occurring just when wholeness seemed on the horizon. Storm clouds are brewing. The doors and windows of academia are imploding from the pressures within and the vacuum above. People are hunkering down, heading for shelter. Yes, this definitely looks like tornado weather.

On the site of a former steel mill—where once the technology of blending coke, iron, slag, oxygen, and fire produced the material that built skyscrapers, monumental towers, bridges, stately ships, and automobiles—today stands a building where clever minds blend technologies and creativity to change the world in new ways. A former "brown field" is now adorned with color. A red-tail hawk perches directly above my office. The ETC is an embodiment of *new* steel. I can't think of any better homage to Andrew Carnegie. As long as I am around, the ETC will remain the Dream Fulfillment Factory. I can't think of any better homage to Randy Pausch.

Acknowledgments

I owe a tremendous debt of gratitude to Pamela Horn from Sterling Innovation. It was her idea to capture and convey the story behind the Carnegie Mellon Entertainment Technology Center (a.k.a. "Dream Fulfillment Factory") and to get the "right brain" perspective on those incredible early years when Randy Pausch and I were crafting this dream.

I would like to thank Joelle Herr and Laura Ross, who so diligently edited the book and provided insightful and astute suggestions and criticism.

I express heartfelt and lifelong gratitude for having a patient and brilliant wife, Jan Grice. She is the smartest person I know. Her commentary, edits, and criticism made this a better book and helped me understand more about myself. Ultimately, I do this as much for my daughter, Olivia, as anyone.

I wish to acclaim publicly the students, staff, and faculty from the ETC. Over the years they have proven to be the most magical group of students and colleagues anyone could ask for. Their greatest gift to me has been an unending fountain of youth. They are the reason I have such great hope for the future.

While I contend everyone's greatest years should reside in front of them, I would like to hail and celebrate the six years Randy Pausch and I spent cheek-by-jowl building the ETC. It was a labor of love in more ways than one. We gave birth to an idea, an instantiation of how education could be, and while the process featured more than its fair share of labor pains, grunts, groans, and pushing, the baby we produced was—and remains—beautiful.

About the DVD

The DVD included with this book contains a synthetic interview with the author, which allows you to "ask" him more than 200 questions related to material referenced in the book. The questions are arranged by subject matter and appear in a drop-down menu—just select the one you want to ask, and the author will answer. Ask as many as you want. In addition, your cursor will indicate whether an item or artifact shown onscreen is interactive. Just click and discover.

If there is a question you would like the author to answer that is not on the list, please feel free to send an email to thedon@cmu.edu so that we may consider it for inclusion on forthcoming DVD releases.

This DVD is an interactive disc compatible with Windows and Mac OS operating systems. It is not an audio book, nor is it a movie to be played in your television's DVD player. On a PC, run Don-SI.exe. On a Mac, run Don-SI.app. The program can be run directly from the disc, or you may drag the application files to your computer and run from the hard drive. Note that 4.1 GB of space is necessary to copy the files to your computer. For slower-running machines, run DonSIlowres.

System Requirements:

Windows XP/VISTA	*MAC OS X*
CPU: 1 GHz	*CPU: Speed equal to or greater than 1.8 GHz*
RAM: 1.5 GB	*RAM: 1024 MB*
DVD ROM	*DVD ROM*

The synthetic interview was created by John Dessler, Krishna Prandavada, and Ralph Vituccio of the Carnegie Mellon Entertainment Technology Center.

About the Author

Don Marinelli is a tenured professor of drama and arts management at Carnegie Mellon University and is also the executive producer of the Entertainment Technology Center (ETC), which he cofounded with colleague Randy Pausch in 1998. He has speaking engagements all over the world but calls Pittsburgh, Pennsylvania, home, where he lives with his wife, Jan.

Photo by Juleigh DeCarlo